Dance

GOD'S HOLY PURPOSE

Ann Stevenson

Treasure House

An Imprint of

Destiny Image® **Publishers, Inc.**
P.O. Box 310
Shippensburg, PA 17257-0310

"For where your treasure is, there will your heart be also"
(Matthew 6:21).

ISBN 10: 0-7684-2441-0
ISBN 13: 978-0-7684-2441-6

For Worldwide Distribution
Printed in the U.S.A.

1 2 3 4 5 6 7 8 9 / 10 09 08 07

This book and all other Destiny Image, Revival Press, MercyPlace, Fresh Bread, Destiny Image Fiction, and Treasure House books are available at Christian bookstores and distributors worldwide.

For a U.S. bookstore nearest you, call **1-800-722-6774**.
For more information on foreign distributors, call **717-532-3040**.
Or reach us on the Internet: **www.destinyimage.com**

Acknowledgments

On February 4, 1992, I cried out loud to God concerning this book, completely uncertain of what was ahead. I desperately needed a clear word from God to confirm whether this book was an aspiration of my own or if it was truly a work of the Spirit. At that moment my Bible fell open to the following verses—even though they were entirely new to me:

> *...the Lord made me understand in writing by His hand upon me, even all the works of this pattern. ...Be strong and of good courage, and do it: fear not, nor be dismayed: for the Lord God, even my God, will be with thee; He will not fail thee, nor forsake thee, until thou hast finished all the work for the service of the house of the Lord. ...and there shall be with thee for all manner of workmanship every willing skilful man, for any manner of service...* (1 Chronicles 28:19-21).

I began to obey this Word and just "do it." God wonderfully and mercifully unfolded the truth of this prophecy before my eyes as He wrote this book through me and provided every willing and skillful person for every manner of service.

I'd like to express my thanks to my precious Teacher who lives within me—my best Friend, my Lord, my Father, my Savior.

Thank You for gracing and trusting me with something as precious as a ministry in the restoration of dance.

To my husband, Jim, thank you for imparting life and strength to me through your awesome, unconditional love, which so undergirds me in this work for the service of the House of the Lord. You are my best gift from God. You truly are the wind beneath my wings.

To Bethany NyKamp, "Miss Bethany." Without you, our school of worship and dance, "Restored to Glory Dance Ministry," would have eventually closed its doors as God called me out to travel, teach, and write. You have stood by my side with the strength of a lion, and with a faithfulness and wisdom that can only come from one who is called and anointed of God to this ministry. We have stood the test of time together since 1987. You are my Elisha. I am so proud of you and honored that God chose you to walk beside me and war with me on a daily basis.

To Peggy Alberda, "Miss Peggy," Director of "Restored to Glory Dance Ministry" in Indiana. You are my sister and my best friend in this world. I respect you more than you could ever know. You have walked with me from day one in this ministry and your words of encouragement and wisdom have strengthened and enabled me to continue. You are a foundation stone and treasure to the Kingdom of God in the restoration of dance to the glory of God.

To Suzie Lutz, Susan Ulstad, Marge Carter, and Grace Inman for truly hearing and sharing the cries of my heart in the early years and even to this day. I love you!

To my mentors, Dr. Fuchsia Pickett and Dr. Judson Cornwall, *"rulers of the king's work, [who] offered willingly"* (1 Chron. 29:6b). Thank you, Judson (Dad), for the selfless hours that you spent with this manuscript, for all that you have taught me, and most of all, for your precious fatherly love. And Fuchsia, it has been an honor to receive your personal help and your words of encouragement; they have made all the difference!

To Laura Irvine and MaryEllen Toeppner, God only knows your selfless, faithful, behind-the-scenes hours of transcribing. I couldn't have done it without you!

To all the pastors, too numerous to mention, who have graciously opened their doors and pulpits, allowing the gift of dance to blossom and grow.

To Reverend Dan Gardner, for allowing me to spread my wings. You've done more than you'll ever know.

To Janny Grein, for demonstrating the anointing and helping me take my first steps.

To Charlotte Baker, Valerie Henery, and Randall Bane, for taking a personal interest in this work and blessing me with your love.

Finally, to the hundreds of dancers and especially the staff members of Restored to Glory Dance Ministry here in Michigan and in Indiana, you have enabled the vision of the restoration of dance to God's glory to become physically manifest to the delight and pleasure of the Lord. Thank you for your faithfulness and many years of devotion.

Endorsements

Balanced, practical, insightful, inspiring. Ann shares not only from professional expertise but from a heart that burns with passion for Jesus. Her entire life exudes a zeal to equip believers in true worship that involves the whole person—body, soul, and spirit. I commend this book wholeheartedly.

Bob Sorge
Author and Oasis House Ministries

The first and great commandment is to love God with all your strength—which involves our bodies. God delights in full-bodied worship. Discover the joy of loving God with all your strength as you read this book. Let your "body talk" in dance and find new ways to express yourself in worship. I recommend this book and Ann Stevenson as a key resource for your research on the theology of the dance. It is the spiritual principles that will bring spiritual results in your dance before the Lord.

Lamar Boschman

Dance, written by Ann Stevenson, an accomplished dancer and dance instructor, is vibrant and full of life. It does not teach a method of dancing; rather, it is a challenge to the ministry of the dance. It is scripturally sound, exegetic, and experiential. It is practical rather than theoretical. Not a book exclusively for dancers, this is a book we all need to read.

Dr. Judson Cornwall
Author, teacher, worshiper

In this book, *Dance*, Ann Stevenson has presented one of the best, most balanced, and well researched books on the subject of restored dance. Ann is a gifted teacher with a keen insight into her subject. I recommend this book as required reading to the serious searcher after truth; and I consider this to be an excellent teaching tool.

Dr. Charlotte E. Baker
Teacher, author

Dance is a compelling revelation of one of the glorious expressions of worship that God is restoring to the Church today—the dance. Ann Stevenson presents the use of this controversial subject with biblical illumination and balance. Ann's heartfelt writing rises out of a deep, personal relationship with God and from many years of ministry experience. Having been personally ministered to by Ann and her dance team, I can attest to the validity of her anointed ministry. This book will help believers more clearly realize God's desire to restore—with balance and care—a greater glory to His Church through the dance.

Dan Gardner
Minister of Music and Worship
Zion Evangelistic Temple, Troy, Michigan
Writer and Hosanna Integrity Music Worship Leader

Contents

~

PERSONAL DANCE STUDY JOURNAL:
Principles and Practice

Foreword

This book is long overdue. It is an excellent presentation, explanation, revelation, and defense for the restoration of the fine art of dancing unto the King of kings in the Church.

The fine arts were not discovered and brought forth by satan, nor by any of his workers. Creativity does not belong to works of satan, but to God. God is the Creator, and He created every expression of art, beauty, and splendor. Therefore the fine arts were created by our God and are to be brought forth in the Church, the Body of Christ.

Because of tradition, the religious laws of man's legalism, and denominationalism, the art of dance for the King was stolen by the enemy. It is glorious to know God is restoring everything that satan, the thief, has stolen and desecrated. The arts are being restored in beauty and honor unto our God and in the highest expressions of worship. Dance is a part of that restoration.

Ann has so ably presented in her book, *Dance*, a sound, scholarly, biblical study of the dance that is much needed by all who are seeking to move into a freer, higher expression of worship. It will be especially helpful for those whom God is calling to lead His people into this realm of worship.

I recognized the call of God to the dance ministry in Ann, and I have supported and encouraged her to follow her calling and to write this book that she has wanted so much to bring to the Body of Christ. I am very impressed with the final manuscript of this much needed revelation to the Body of Christ.

Dr. Fuchsia T. Pickett

Preface

In the challenge of this journey called life, lays a secret path between man and God called worship. This mysteriously spiritual encounter is our destiny and there is a primal need within every man to embrace God through the intimacy and surrender of true worship. A cry of the heart to touch God in worship is zealously sweeping the earth in this end-time restoration and preparation for the King of Glory. The Church is passionately hungry for truth and divine direction that will teach and enable them in this call to worship.

Thousands of books have been and are being written as this revelation is being led by the Spirit of God calling us to Himself. Step by step we have experienced this restoration taking place and slowly but surely as the flesh surrenders, more and more freedom is visibly noticeable in the Church worldwide. Large international worship conferences gather men and women from every corner of the earth with a driving force that will not be quenched.

Churches big and small are hosting worship conferences from one end of the earth to the other hungrily seeking truth and direction from the heart of God. As this driving zeal of the Spirit is compelling us forward, the Church has rightfully responded by thoroughly searching the Scriptures for hidden keys that will unlock God's divine and original intension, direction, and biblical instructions for worship. Surprisingly in this intense searching of Scriptures we have discovered an unexpected, often unwanted, yet undeniable key element of worship.

This element is *dance*. There are those who have rejected the command of God concerning dance in the church and those who have embraced it with an excited zeal, yet lacking in the knowledge of its divine order. Either way, the restoration of dance has suffered violent warfare and no matter how elaborate our dance garments, banners, and streamers may appear, we are still in the early pioneer stages of restoration in light of the fullness that lies ahead.

Dancers are pressing through many obstacles and dimensions of being misunderstood by even the most passionate and educated leaders in worship. I thank God for the brave company of worship dancers, who are swimming upstream—facing the harshest of elements in both the natural and spiritual realm. The enemy is vehemently opposed to the dance being taken out of his worldly kingdom while being restored to the glory of its rightful purpose in the Kingdom of God. Discerning and withstanding the whiles of this ancient foe in battle requires maturity, wisdom, and experiential knowledge which this book effectively helps to promote. This war will not be won without the inevitable spiritual battle which is ultimately not about the dance per se but about the fullness of worship in its entirety as God designed it.

We must realize that corporate worship in the Church will never complete or accomplish its original purpose to the satisfaction of God's heart without the divine element of dance functioning in its proper place and according to the order of His Word. We still have much not only to learn but to actively apply when it comes to dance functioning and accomplishing its highest created purpose. This book, *Dance: God's Holy Purpose* sets a high standard for the education and restoration of dance according the Word of God. Whether you are a skeptic, a devout congregational worshiper or one who is called to the ministry and priesthood of the dancer, *Dance: God's Holy Purpose* has something for everyone.

Originally released in 1998, this book has brought revelation, freedom, and Godly order to countless worshipers worldwide as readers have enthusiastically responded with letters of thanks from even the most remote corners of the earth. The biblical principles and truths outlined in this book are timeless and we have at best only begun to touch the hem of the garment which they represent.

Ann Stevenson
Restored to Glory Dance Ministry School of Worship

Introduction

The disciples asked Jesus in Matthew 24:3, *"...what shall be the sign of Thy coming, and of the end of the world?"* His answer to them reads like today's headlines—persecution, hatred, false prophets, wars, famine, pestilence, earthquakes, etc. Yet, Scripture also tells us, *"...that He may send Jesus, the Christ appointed for you, whom heaven must receive* [retain] *until the **period of restoration of all things** about which God spoke by the mouth of His holy prophets..."* (Acts 3:20-21 NASB).

As the signs of the times reveal that the end is drawing near, so must the restoration of all things as spoken by the mouths of the prophets take place before the return of Christ. My heart is filled with a message of simple truths, which I desire to share with all who would have ears to hear. These truths concern the restoration of a precious gift from our Creator, and this gift is dance. The Body of Christ has been deceived and robbed of this gift having its proper place in the Church as a powerful tool of ministry in worship, warfare, and celebration.

Satan has successfully convinced many Christians that dance is carnal in nature. Some believe, without question, that there is no place for dance within the Church today. This is an understandable point of view, for the only example of dance previously known to most has been that of a worldly nature. With the world as our standard, we have most often witnessed a distorted, perverted version of what God originally created for a pure and holy purpose.

God has placed a desire in my heart to see this gift restored in purity to His glory, honor, and power. It is time for God's original intent and purpose for creating dance to be taught in balance and in accordance with God's Word within the Church at large. I have witnessed a great deal of imbalance in the Church, which has resulted in two major extremes. On the one hand, there are those who are taking a stand for what seems comfortable, proper, and trouble-free, concluding that the safest policy is to have no dance at all. Their philosophy seems to be, "If you want to avoid the risk of drowning, don't even put your toe in the water." This is a group that I want to stir up and inspire to break the chains and bondages of religion and the traditions of man. With them, I see myself at the reins saying, "Come on, let's go."

On the other hand, there are those who are experiencing an "anything goes," or over-zealousness, in the dance without any sound teaching according to God's Word. This acting in zeal without knowledge can bring great confusion to an already skeptical, wounded Church. Let's be careful not to take just one portion of Scripture on the dance, such as, *"Let them praise His name in the dance"* (Ps. 149:3a), and run with it. A little knowledge can be dangerous. To this group, I see myself pulling back on the reins, saying, "Whoa! Slow down!" This group seems to have no knowledge of the dangers of deep waters, and are jumping into an area over their heads where they won't know how to swim or even stay afloat.

We are living in a time when things are moving very quickly in the physical world as well as in the spiritual realm of the Kingdom of God. This can be exciting and dangerous at the same time. In today's generation, our culture has trained us to desire and expect instant gratification; however, this is the opposite of the training necessary for developing the Christ-like character we as the Church were created to be formed into.

This rushed training nourishes and satisfies our carnal nature, while enforcing and adding fuel to the already raging battle between soul and spirit. The dance that God longs to see restored is one of spirit and truth, not flesh and soul.

Many pitfalls await to ensnare the Church, which can bring discouragement, doubt, and fear. Many churches start out with a bang, in a hurry to experience the fullness of what God has for us in dance, only to crash and burn shortly thereafter. Another victory for the enemy is gained as these churches often never want to have anything to do with dance again. We must realize that the true restoration of dance in holiness and purity cannot be rushed.

> *Desire without knowledge is not good, and to be over-hasty is to sin and miss the mark* (Proverbs 19:2 AMP).

Another important truth concerning God's order in the dance is that God will always begin by redeeming and restoring the man before dealing with that man's gifts or ministry. He cares more about who we are in Him than what we think we can do for Him.

Obviously, before one considers the dance, he or she must have a true revelation of and a relationship with Jesus Christ as Lord and Savior. It would be a vain and empty process to attempt to go through the motions of worshiping a God that you have never known or loved. Unless there has been an inner transformation of the spirit-man, dance used in the capacity of praise and worship is nothing more than physical exercise to Christian music. God is far more concerned with the re-creation of your spirit than the physical recreation of your body. It is not the restoration of dance itself that pleases the heart of God, but it is the restoration of dance that is birthed as an overflowing expression of love, joy, victory, and thankfulness through those who are spiritually restored in Christ. Therefore we can say, "God seeks not the restoration of dance but the dance of the restored."

At this point in time, as we seek to find success in repossessing this land we call *dance*, there is a great spiritual warfare against its restoration to the fullness of God's original intent and purpose. The goal of this book is to cut through the deceptions of the enemy with the sword of the Spirit, to reveal the truth, and to clearly expose his lies as we renew our minds according to the beauty and order of God's holy Word.

The unfolding of revelation concerning the dance did not come quickly or easily to me. The transformation of the renewing of my carnal mind was a process that began long before I was aware of it, as God's pre-ordained call on my life became progressively revealed.

From the time I started dance lessons at the age of 3, and up to the age of 25, all I ever knew of dance was what the world had to offer. The idea of connecting dance with God, church, or worship was the farthest thing from my mind. I was raised in a very traditional church. I was instructed that church was a very serious matter. The priest's voice would echo through the microphone and bounce off the high cathedral ceilings, creating an atmosphere of power and majesty as he spoke—mostly in Latin. Even quietly laughing with my brothers and sisters during a service was considered a sin. When I was young, that seemed to be a perpetual sin of mine—I knelt numerous times before the priest in confession saying, "Bless me, Father, for I have sinned; I laughed in church."

I would not have considered dancing in church any more than I would have considered roller-skating around the altar during Mass. Other than singing a few complicated hymns, a dead silence surrounded the entire congregation each week. The only hands that were lifted at my church were by those who periodically checked their watches to see how much longer it would be before we could all go home.

This was all I ever knew of praise and worship, and I'm sure there are many who can relate to my experience. Quietness meant holiness, and from my earliest days, this religious tradition of what was good and acceptable behavior before God became deeply ingrained in me. I must admit that through these experiences I developed a deep respect for the house of God and the gathering place called the sanctuary. Somewhere along the line, my family went from never missing a Sunday to not going to church at all. At first, I thought I wouldn't go to Heaven because of this. But, much to my relief, some kind person along the way explained to me that since I wasn't old enough to drive myself to church, God would understand. I never stopped loving, respecting, and praying to God every night, even though God still seemed very far off. I just went through the motions that I had been taught. They were all that I knew. I never questioned whether something might be missing. How could I miss something that I never had?

My spiritual life remained the same as I grew older and eventually married. My husband, Jim, and I had our first child in 1977, and everything was wonderful. When our son Ashley was three years old, something began to happen inside me. All the circumstances in my life were seemingly perfect. I had a wonderful, happy family. I had my own business in which I was teaching dance, and we were building a new home. Yet something was wrong; these things weren't enough. It was as though God's finger was pressing upon my heart. In my spirit I could hear Him calling me by name, "Ann...Ann...I want you now." I had never felt this way before. God was talking to me—not just me to Him. His voice was so strong and real; I knew that I had to respond in some way.

I decided to visit a church that a friend of ours attended. It was just a little place called Calvary Fellowship. The people were very friendly from the first time I walked in. Everyone was smiling and acting so happy. When I entered the sanctuary, people were talking, shaking hands, hugging, and get this, even laughing! Yes, they were laughing in the sanctuary! All my religious foundations were beginning to shake.

I was very suspicious. When they began to sing, it was loud! They smiled and clapped. Many raised their hands, and a few people even kind of danced up and down in place. When the song ended, there wasn't dead silence. People said things like, "Thank You, Lord"; "I love You, Lord Jesus"; and "Praise God"! Some people even went so far as to actually cry. *What were they crying about?* I couldn't believe what I was seeing. This was all very strange to me. I was uncomfortable, and I certainly didn't understand. I had no real personal relationship with God, so how could I possibly understand worship? When the pastor began to talk, I just melted in my seat. He brought the Scriptures to life. I could actually understand the Bible the way he explained it.

For the next few months, my great hunger for God caused me to go to church every Sunday. The Word of God was fulfilling an inner need and changing the entire focus and direction of my life. I remember that it was during this time when I privately decided to dedicate my entire life to serving God. I prayed that He would be glorified in and through everything I did.

Due to this decision, I became confused about my dancing. I could not understand how it could have any part in serving God, bringing salvation to others, or glorifying God in any way. I enthusiastically decided that it would be best for me to give up my dance studio and find out what it was that God really wanted me to do. I pictured myself working in the kitchen of the church with some of the other women I had been watching and admiring in their godly service to the Lord. My husband was very willing to support whatever decision I felt was right for me.

Time moved on, and I never missed a service; however, I always arrived one hour late. Why one hour late? Because the first hour was all that praise and worship stuff. I just couldn't understand why grown men and women would act like that in church. It seemed foolish to me. Whoever heard of singing songs for a whole hour every Sunday? Why, when I was young our entire church service barely lasted 45 minutes—and that was too long.

One week our pastor said something about always coming in late, and I knew he meant me. Out of respect for him I began to arrive on time. That is when something new started to happen within me. I fell so in love with God that such worshipful music with words that expressed what I felt in my heart nearly brought me to tears. Notice, I said *nearly*. I was not about to allow myself to express my private inner emotions by any revealing outward expression. I firmly believed that this was inappropriate behavior in church, and besides, whoever heard of crying in church, except maybe at a funeral? I was not going to allow myself to look foolish like some of those other people.

A battle was going on inside me. I didn't understand that with all my heart I needed to do the very thing I was created to do, which is to worship God. Yet the traditions I had been taught all my life and had accepted without question told me that such outward expressions in the house of God were out of order and foolish. A painful war was taking place in my spirit, and it only became worse.

Every week, everything within me wanted to express worship to God, but I couldn't do it. I just couldn't. A voice inside me would say, "You'll look foolish. If you raise your hands or cry, everyone will look at you. And look at them, don't they look silly? Grown men and women acting so emotional. Wouldn't you be embarrassed?" The voice went on and on and gave me every reason under the sun why I shouldn't or couldn't participate. But my spirit was being wooed by God. He was calling and longing for me to commune with Him in worship and be set free from the chains of tradition that bound me and kept us apart.

One Sunday night we had a service unlike anything I had ever be-fore experienced. After a full hour of intense worship that was heavy with the presence of God, God was touching many people. It was an awesome thing, and I just stood there ready to break. Yet I was still fighting and holding back my true feelings with every ounce of strength within me. If the musicians had stopped after the first hour, I may have succeeded in suppressing my emotions. But, praise God, they went on for another hour.

This was more than I could handle. God literally wrapped His arms of love around me. I felt the warmth of His love, and it was like nothing I'd ever known before. It was so real, yet I still couldn't respond to Him. I felt as if I was about to explode. Finally, I could resist Him no longer. The anointing of God broke the yoke that I never knew I had. I began to weep and raise my hands to the Father. One of the songs declared, "I draw near to you, my Father, I draw near to you with all my heart, Oh my Father, when I'm with you I find I am blessed. Oh my Father, Oh my Father, Oh Lord, my God, my Father, my Father."[1] I sang those words with real understanding, and my Father and I truly embraced one another for the first time.

Later that same night I had a dream. I saw men and women acting out a worshipful drama dance that had a strong message of salvation. They brought great worship and glory to God through their movements. In the dream I could also see people watching the dancers. As they watched, they wept and were being powerfully ministered to deep in their spirits. Having been a dance teacher and choreographer for 11 years, I had created many dances, but this was entirely different. It had power and meaning that was beyond anything I had ever imagined.

At that time, I had never heard of such a thing as dancing for the Lord. I was a baby Christian, and everything was new and strange to me. Although this was a prophetic dream from the Lord, I did not know it at the time. I only knew that somehow I was no longer quite so sure about giving up dancing, and I decided to put the decision on hold. I told no one about the dream; I just kept it in my heart. As I look back, that was the wise thing to do, for it wasn't yet time to pursue it.

This dream was the very first step of God's plan, for He was gradually bringing me into an understanding of His original purpose for the creation of the dance. My husband built a beautiful dance studio for me in our new home, and God began, slowly and progressively, to make changes in my dancing. I could no longer use music that had once been acceptable to me. I no longer felt comfortable with certain movements I had once used. God began developing a desire in my heart to use my dance skills to glorify Him.

Because I had students who represented a variety of religious backgrounds, as well as some with no religious background at all, I decided to make the theme of our annual dance recital about Christmas so I could use songs about Christ without offending anyone. God was doing a work in me. He was progressively developing His master plan for my life, and I didn't even know it.

God's work in my spirit continued through the birth of our second child, Abigail Elizabeth. God was building a strong foundation in me according to His Word concerning my role as a wife and a mother. Although ministry was the farthest thing from my mind, during those years I felt as though I carried in my spirit a hidden treasure concerning the dance that was stirring and preparing to be birthed.

One afternoon, I was praying, praising, and communing with God in my journal when I wrote something that was not my own thought: "You must not faint easily; in this I have chosen you." Nothing like this had ever happened to me before, nor had I ever heard of such a thing. I dropped my pen and began to pace and pray. The Spirit was so strong. God was speaking directly to me. As I returned to my journal, I received a clear, direct prophecy by the Spirit of the Lord, which has continued to unfold in my life ever since.

Throughout that following week, God deposited an understanding deep into my spirit that He had created me for and was calling me to a ministry in dance. The measure of the Lord that came mightily upon me that day is still with me, and nothing can ever take that away from me. I was called and anointed by God—like David was when, as a child, he was anointed and called to be king: *"Then Samuel took the horn of oil and anointed him in the midst of his brothers; and the spirit of the Lord came mightily upon David from that day forward..."* (1 Sam. 16:13 NASB).

I had never before thought of dance as a ministry. It even sounded funny to me, but I loved to dance, and I loved the Lord, so what could be more perfect? Although God had warned me in that prophecy concerning spiritual warfare and that I was not to doubt or faint, I thought, *This is going to be great! Why would I ever doubt or faint?* I had no idea of the preparatory trials and testings that were yet to come. And come they would—in God's perfect timimg.

From that day forward, my life was not the same. Immediately God's Word opened to me concerning dance, and He began to progressively reveal to me His original intent and purpose for the creation of dance. I began to write these things down, feeling strongly in my spirit that these revelations would someday become a book.

Back at the dance studio, my love for Jesus could no longer be contained. The zeal of God consumed me, and it was contagious. My secular dance classes had become a hothouse of God's glory. My students had always looked up to me as their teacher, and now, as the life of Christ poured through me, they soaked it up like dry sponges. Many were saved. One week an entire class of teenagers approached me before class. The expressions on their faces were very serious as they asked me if I would please pray the prayer of salvation with them that week. As I prayed with them, they embraced one another and wept.

The anointing flowed. The presence of God in the dance studio was like a cloud of fog that hovered there.

My dance classes were not the only place where things were changing. Doors began to open for me to dance in many different churches and public places. The response of the people was greater than I had ever expected. I had danced all my life, but this was something completely different. God was doing something so meaningful and powerful that as I danced, people were deeply touched by Him to the point of weeping and receiving spiritual revelation and inner healing. Although I still had very little understanding about this new realm of dance, God was opening doors and I was walking—no, running—through them. I was swept away in the zeal of it all.

In April 1984, I was given the opportunity of ministering in dance at a couple of meetings in Oklahoma. One I will never forget was an international intercessory prayer conference in Tulsa. My friend Janny Grein, with whom I was spending the week, has a well-known music ministry and was leading the service on worship and spiritual warfare that evening. I had ministered in the dance several times before with Janny's anointed singing, and the Lord had been using her to open doors for me as I started out in ministry. Before the meeting that evening we agreed that I would sit with the congregation and enjoy the evening rather than minister in a choreographed dance.

As it turned out, God had a different plan. The people at this conference had been in prayer meetings for three days, and as they congregated, they were more than ready to worship. When the worship started, the Spirit of God fell thick over us. The presence of God was moving powerfully when I heard Him call. He wanted me on stage, and He said that He was "going to minister through me in the dance."

All the reasons why I could not do that flooded my mind. I wasn't wearing my dance dress; I had never danced before a group of people without a prearranged choreographed dance; and Janny was playing new songs I had never heard before. Everything was wrong, but it was unmistakably the Lord, so I answered, "OK Lord, but, please confirm this through Janny." Within five minutes, right in the middle of a song, Janny called me out of the crowd onto the stage, saying, "Ann, you've got to get up here on this stage."

That night was a whole new experience for me. It was the very first time I had ever danced before the Lord in front of people solely by the momentary inspiration of the Holy Spirit. I had never felt the power of God like that before. I literally, physically felt the anointing rushing through me and out my fingertips like water blasting through a hose as I stretched my hands out over the people, interpreting the word of the songs through dance. After the meeting, the response of the congregation was overwhelming. People followed us down the hall and out the door to our car with testimonies of how the anointing of God had powerfully touched them each in different ways.

As God took me to the mountain top, allowing me to taste of the glory that was possible through dance, it seemed as though a red carpet was being rolled out before me, as I danced down it. The presence of God had permeated my life. All I wanted was to know Him more and more. My spirit cried out daily to God, "I want to become all that You have created me to be. Cleanse me, mold me, change me. Lord, make me a golden vessel. Have Your perfect will in my life. Oh God, do whatever it takes."

When I prayed these prayers I had no idea what I was asking. It reminds me of the mother of the sons of Zebedee as she approached Jesus in Matthew 20:21-22 (NASB), asking Jesus if her two sons could sit, one on the right and the other on the left of Him in His Kingdom. His reply to her and her sons was, *"You do not know what you are asking for. Are you able to drink the cup that I am about to drink?"* The cup Jesus spoke of is the cup of suffering and death. He suffered and died for us so that we could live. We must, in turn, die to our own will so that He can live through us.

I understood the principles of death to self. I had heard and read these truths many times, but it would take experiential knowledge for these principles to become true revelation in my heart. It is a glorious and wonderful thing to be birthed into a deeper realm in Christ, but to whom much is given, much is required. And where there is a birth, there must first be labor.

Suddenly my red carpet came to an end. I danced from the mountain top down into the depths of the valley of the shadow of death. As my spirit groaned and continually cried out for transformation, it seemed as though God's refiner's fire had come into my life almost overnight. This was my personal time of intense preparation and training while my Father held me in the palm of His hand and intimately close to His heart. God's plans required me to experience the truth of Christ's words, *"...he that loseth his life for My sake shall find it"* (Matt. 10:39).

My loving and merciful Father guided me step by step through a very long and difficult time of darkness in order to bring me into a dimension of His glorious light that I would never have otherwise known. I didn't dance or teach for the next three years as God worked something of eternal value deep within me. He brought me to a place where I didn't care if I ever danced again. I didn't care if I became a cleaning woman who scrubbed public toilets for a living or a ditch digger who labored daily in the hot sun. I only wanted to know Him and feel His pleasure in me as I submitted to His will—whatever it might be. He birthed in me a burning desire for intimacy in Him beyond what I had ever imagined possible.

My personal quest is for the depth of the heights of His glory. I share this book with you not as a dancer or as a dance teacher, but a worshiper. Without Jesus, dance means nothing whatsoever to me. Yet as an effective means of communication and expression of my love to my God, it is a special, hidden treasure whose power, beauty, and mystery must be unveiled.

Dance has many different levels of expression, with something for everyone. It is the desire of God's heart to have a people who will humbly and sincerely worship Him, not only with singing and musical instruments, but in the beautiful language of physical expression through our bodies. This pure and holy form of worship is precious to God. It cannot and will not be left in the twisted hands of the enemy.

The restoration of the dance is presently being birthed in the Body of Christ, as God is unfolding and revealing His original purpose for its creation. This book was never intended specifically for dancers. From the very beginning the intent of my heart was that this book be written for the Body of Christ at large with a foremost desire to see it reach the hands of pastors, worship leaders, and dance leaders. My intention is that this book would lay a basic solid foundation of truth and holiness that dance may be restored in the Church to the glory, honor, and pleasure of our God. I pray that this book will promote a new realm of worship within you that you may reach out and touch God as never before. I pray that you will experience a release of your spirit to worship our Father in the manner in which He desires, delights in, and worthily deserves.

ENDNOTE

1. "My Father," by Robert Carefoot. Used by permission of composer.

CHAPTER 1

The Dance on Trial

Imagine with me a type of spiritual court case being tried in the minds of a group of individuals who are collectively known as the Church. Within this group, a matter of much controversy has emerged. The subject now in question is that of the validity and function *of dance in the church*. Through the ages, satan has systematically presented a cleverly convincing case before these people with the intent of preventing the emergence of even the thought of such a thing as dance in the church.

In the minds of a people honestly seeking holiness, dance has appeared to be anything and everything but holy. The ungodly representation of the perverse, physical evidence witnessed by this and past generations has built a strong case for classifying it as a worldly practice. As dance functioned and flourished in the camp of the enemy over the years, the Church believed without dispute that it was right where it belonged. Dance became virtually nonexistent in the church as this convincing evidence blocked the thoughts of the Church as well as blinded eyes of its members. God's original intent for creating the dance unfortunately seemed lost.

Satan's deceptive strategy appeared to be progressing according to plan. The word *strategy*, comes from the word *strategum*, meaning, "a cleverly contrived trick or scheme for gaining an end." Although it may seem that the enemy's trick had deceived the Church, God always has a strategy that infinitely outweighs and outwits that of the enemy. For example, it may have seemed obvious to satan that his plan for Christ's death on the Cross would achieve his ultimate victory; but, as we all know, this one event accomplished satan's ultimate and eternal defeat. As we parallel this thought with the issue of dance, we must remember that what appears obvious is not always true.

Concerning the issue of dance and its validity, original purpose, and function in the Church, we still have a long road ahead in accomplishing its full restoration. Not only is there a spiritual war to be waged in repossessing what rightfully belongs to us, but we have perhaps an even greater war to be waged within our own minds to bring unity, understanding, and balance to this controversial area in the Church.

Is the dance on trial? Yes, it certainly is, and because of our free will, you, the reader, stand in the role of a member of the jury (the Church). In this spiritual court battle, the role of the prosecution is played by *satan, the accuser of the brethren*. And in defense of the dance, with the intent to rightly divide the truth, we have *the Word of God*, which is faithful and true.

The Prosecution: Satan, the Accuser of the Brethren

Noah Webster's First Edition of an American Dictionary of the English Language gives us three definitions of *prosecute*. Prosecute means:

1. To seek to obtain by legal process.

   The prosecution knows all too well the strengths and weaknesses of this jury. He knows his only hope is to appear to abide by the legal process of presenting truth as it is found in the law of the Word of God. He knows it is the whole truth and nothing but the truth they seek; therefore, he must disguise his deceptions in nothing other than the truth. Jurors beware, for the prosecution has an unmatched reputation of expertise tactics in twisting the truth of the law to seemingly support his deceptions. To illustrate this, it would be wise to note that rat poison can consist of 98 percent corn; it is the 2 percent arsenic that poisons.

2. To accuse of some crime or breech of law.

   Remember, in this particular case, it is not the Church that has been accused by satan. He knows better; he needs them as his jury. It is the dance itself that he accuses of breaking the scriptural laws of righteousness, holiness, and morality. Remember, satan uses the law itself to accuse, but not according to the truth. Our jury must be as wise as serpents, matching wits, in order to discern the truth in this case.

3. Suing for a right or claim.

   Satan, the prosecutor, seeks to obtain and possess all rights and claim to the dance by the process of accusing it of being unholy and immoral, therefore having no legal or moral role in the functioning of the church service.

The Defense: The Word of God, Faithful and True

Once again, using Noah Webster's dictionary, we see two principle definitions of the word *defend*.

1. To strike, thrust or drive off; to repel, to drive from, to thrust back, to oppose, resist, to defend against an assailant or the approach of evil or danger with the purpose of maintaining one's own claim.

   Spiritually, I envision the dance in its purest form being, for the most part, *out of view* and unrecognizable to the Body of Christ due to the fact that it is under attack. I see it as covered with and being attacked by large, black birds of prey. Each bird is squawking, flapping its wings and struggling for a turn to peck and devour, intending to disguise and destroy the original God-given purity of the dance. Throughout this case, the Word of God will strike, thrust back, and drive off the attack of the enemy in an effort to maintain the Church's claim to the dance. The defense desires to see the purity of the dance which has so deceptively been taken *out of view*, be brought *back into view*, so that the Church may begin to understand God's original intent and purpose for its creation.

2. To vindicate; to defend the reputation of by *argument or force*; that which disproves a charge or accusation.

    Argument: Although the reputation of the dance has been severely damaged, its vindication is now taking place in the Church. As we saw, the definition of *defend* means to vindicate, to defend the reputation of a thing by force or argument. Both are necessary in the balanced restoration of the dance. This book deals with the argument side of the issue in the sense of offering sound reasoning and evidence of truth by using the Word of God.

    Force: The other element of defense and vindication is that of force. This aspect of the restoration of dance takes place when it is actively demonstrated in the natural by those who will courageously, humbly, and obediently respond to the promptings of the Holy Spirit, daring to release through outward expression the inward emotion of their hearts. When this is done in spirit and truth, it is beautifully saturated with the evidence of God's presence. It instantly dispels and disproves all previous charges or accusations against the validity and holiness of dance.

We could talk about dance all day long. We could even come into agreement upon every issue concerning it. But if the demonstration of dance is not made manifest in the natural, it will never be truly restored. Skillful argument is necessary in this process, but there must also be force of action, for *"...the kingdom of heaven suffereth violence, and the violent take it by force"* (Matt. 11:12).

Therefore, the defense will oppose, strike, repel, and drive off the schemes of the enemy through argument (based on the truth of God's Word), and force (as the physical representation of the dance is presented before our God in spirit and truth).

We will now proceed with our spiritual court case as we witness the opening statements of the prosecution and the defense.

Opening Statement of the Prosecution

"Scripture tells us in First John 2:15-16, *'Love not the world, neither the things that are in the world. If any man love the world, the love of the Father is not in him. For all that is in the world, the lust of the flesh, and the lust of the eyes, and the pride of life, is not of the Father, but is of the world.'*

"Dance, since the beginning of time, has been proven beyond the shadow of a doubt to strongly promote the lust of the flesh, the lust of the eyes, and the pride of life. Therefore, dance is not of the Church's Father, but of this world, and rightfully belongs to the ruler of this world, satan. Christians are instructed in the Word of God to not love the world or the things of this world, which includes dance. For if any man loves the world, Scripture tells us that the love of the Father is not in him. Therefore, I ask you, could anything be worth such a risk? Consequently, in keeping with the laws of the heavenly Father, there is no doubt that the Church should have nothing whatsoever to do with this lustful, fleshy, prideful practice known as dance."

Opening Statement for the Defense

"The defense intends to prove, scripturally, beyond the shadow of a doubt, that dance was originally created for the glory, honor, and power of the Lord God Almighty.

"It rightfully was created for His pleasure and it belongs to the Church for its function in warfare, celebration, and the intimate communication of worship. The defense intends to expose the evil schemes, strategy, and motives of the prosecution and reveal the underlying purpose for the prosecution's desperate attempt to deceive and rob the Church concerning the true function of this gift."

The Trial Begins

The word *hearing* in reference to a court case, means "attendance to the facts, testimony, and arguments in a cause between two parties, with a view to a just decision." The prosecution (satan) has had the advantage of presenting his case since the beginning of time. It is now time for the defense (the Word of God) to be heard. Although the defense has the disadvantage of all the preconceived notions and mindsets established by the enemy thus far, the defense stands in complete confidence that God's truth will prevail.

The focus of this trial is to seek a just decision and a godly verdict. *Verdict* comes from the Latin term, *verum dictum*, meaning "true declaration." It is time for the truth concerning the dance to be declared to the Church. You (the church, the reader, the jury) have been given a free will by God to decide for yourself how you feel about the dance. But the true verdict concerning the dance does not depend upon how we, the Church, feel. The truth was decided when God created the dance, and it has been declared to us in the form of God's written Word.

It is our responsibility as individuals to align ourselves with what God says is true, not what the enemy has deceptively manifested in the natural as evidence that exalts itself against the knowledge of God. As this spiritual court case now proceeds, the writings of this book stand as evidence of the defense with the purpose of renewing the mind of the Church according to the Word of God.

CHAPTER 2

~

Renewing Your Mind

In our quest for truth concerning the restoration of dance to the Church, our ultimate answers will not be found in our traditions, history books, and certainly not in the opinions of men. The standard by which all truth is to be measured is none other than the Word of God. These truths are revealed to us through a process the Bible calls "transforming" or "renewing" our mind.

> *And be not conformed to this world: but be ye transformed by the renewing of your mind, that ye may prove what is that good, and acceptable, and perfect, will of God* (Romans 12:2).

The dance is good, acceptable, and perfect according to God's will. Yet, in rejecting the dance because of the distorted view that the world has presented, we are actually conforming to the world. We have allowed our perception and decisions concerning the dance to be shaped and molded by the world's standard.

In seeking to accurately renew our minds concerning this subject, it is helpful to briefly examine the basic beginnings of this rejection and separation of dance from the church.

This subject is examined in greater detail in Chapter 4, The Roots of Corruption.

Man's Rejection

In the earliest days of the Dark Ages, the Christian Church became a state-organized institution that required the membership of every man and woman regardless of the morality or immorality of their behavior. Since involvement in the Christian Church was no longer dependent upon one's relationship with God or upon salvation through Jesus Christ, many pagan practices infiltrated the Church, including lewd and perverted expressions of dance.

To eliminate the dances of pagan perversion, many churches eventually banned all forms of dance, even the previously accepted dances designed specifically for God's praise and worship. To make matters even worse, a deceptive philosophy arose that denounced any practice that resulted in pleasure to the physical body as evil. The leadership that enforced these philosophies undoubtedly believed that they were acting to preserve holiness and purity in the Church. In reality, these leaders fell into a trap of the enemy by establishing traditions that continue to rob the Church of precious gifts designed for God's glory.

Scripture says, *"And be not conformed to this world"* (Rom. 12:2a). The Greek definition of the word *conform* is "to fashion self according to." Therefore, we are not to fashion ourselves according to what the world is doing. Unfortunately, as I stated earlier, this is exactly what has happened. Because of the pagan perversions of dance, the Church fashioned philosophies and traditions in direct opposition to God's Word, allowing the minds of its members to be altered and formed according to the world's actions.

> *To every thing there is a season, and a time to every purpose under the heaven...a time to break down, and a time to build up...a time to mourn, and a time to dance* (Ecclesiastes 3:1-4).

God's original purpose for the dance has been broken down, but it is now the season and the time for its purpose to be revealed and rebuilt. Renewing our mind not only involves the necessary process of rebuilding truth, but there is an exposing and tearing down of false understanding that is just as important. We must be careful not to take a worldly version of dance and mix it with God's holy purpose. Instead, we must begin with a bare foundation and build upward exclusively upon Jesus Christ, the Word of God:

> *For no other foundation can anyone lay than that which is [already] laid, which is Jesus Christ (the Messiah, the Anointed One)* (1 Corinthians 3:11 AMP).

The Amplified Bible renders Romans 12:2, "...*but be transformed* (changed) *by the* [entire] *renewal of your mind....*" The word transformed is the Greek word *meta-morphoo*. This is where we get our word *metamorphose*, which means "to change into a different physical form, especially by supernatural means." In order for dance to be fully restored in holiness, there must be an exclusion of all forms of worldly mixture. We cannot build a holy revelation upon an ungodly foundation. What God wants is a complete metamorphosis, or transformation, of our minds, according to His Word.

How, then, does God instruct us to be transformed? Romans 12:2 says, *"by the renewing of your mind."* The mind is the enemy's targeted area of attack. He has not only convinced many Christians that dance is worldly, but he has planned to rob us of the understanding that it ever belonged to us in the first place. He knew if he could accomplish this, there would be no reason for the Church to pursue the matter, and he could, in turn, possess full control over this powerful, beautiful gift. Satan understands that once a man settles an issue in his mind, it is very difficult to convince him otherwise, especially if that man feels he has chosen what is right in the eyes of God. This type of deception, which I believe has encompassed the issue of dance in the Church, is difficult to expose.

What God Hath Cleansed

The Book of Acts relates a story that beautifully parallels this very issue of renewing our minds and how difficult it can be. We must be sensitive to God. We must not limit Him by the traditions of men; but instead, we must move in obedience to the clearly expressed will of God that is revealed in His Word.

In Acts 10:9-16, Peter was praying when a vision came to him. He saw a great sheet lowered before him. Upon it were all kinds of animals, creeping things, and birds that were considered unholy and ceremonially unclean to eat according to the Jewish laws. Then Peter heard the voice of the Lord say, *"Rise up, Peter, kill, and eat"* (Acts 10:13b AMP). Peter knew it was the Lord, for he answered, *"...No, by no means, Lord; for I have never eaten anything that is common and unhallowed or* [ceremonially] *unclean"* (Acts 10:14 AMP). The Lord spoke a second time, saying, *"What God has cleansed and pronounced clean, do not you defile and profane by regarding and calling common and unhallowed or unclean"* (Acts 10:15b AMP).

It was difficult for Peter's mind to be changed from what he had believed to be right. Although Peter knew it was the voice of the Lord (he responded, *"...by no means, **Lord**..."*), God had to tell him three times! Peter wasn't being rebellious; he just had a difficult time accepting an understanding that differed from what he had settled in his mind to be true. Through a series of events, Peter came to understand the interpretation of the vision. He was to preach the gospel to the Gentiles. This was not an easy message for Peter to receive, for it went against the Jewish law.

Peter understood the great opposition that he would come up against in doing such a thing. At that time, according to Jewish law, it was not permissible for a Jew to keep company with, to visit, come near, or even to speak first to anyone of another nationality. We can all be thankful that Peter's fear of God outweighed his fear of man. And the very next morning, he departed from Caesarea to take the gospel to the Gentiles.

When the other apostles heard what Peter was doing, they "...*found fault with him [separating themselves from him in a hostile spirit, opposing and disputing and contending with him]*" (Acts 11:2 AMP). This had to have been hard on Peter. I believe what finally convinced the other apostles that Peter's actions were God's will was that the Gentiles had also received the manifestation of the Holy Spirit by speaking in tongues when they heard the gospel. Peter said in reference to this, "...*who was I and what power or authority had I to interfere or hinder or forbid or withstand God?*" (Acts 11:17 AMP)

Many parallels can be made between this story and that of the restoration of dance. Consider a few of the following items.

First, Peter had a great deal of difficulty allowing his mind to be renewed concerning what was clean and unclean, even when God spoke directly to him three times. Like Peter, some believers have difficulty receiving dance as something that is clean before the Lord when church tradition has taught them all their lives that all dance is evil and sinful. I understand this, but we must not limit God; we must view dance from God's perspective, as it is portrayed by Him in His Word. God and His Church will not be robbed.

Second, although what God spoke to Peter went against Jewish law, it did not go against the written Word as it had been prophesied by the prophets. The apostle James pointed out in Acts 15:13-17 (AMP),

> ...*Brethren, listen to me. Simeon [Peter] has rehearsed how God first visited the Gentiles, to take out of them a people [to bear and honor] His name. And with this the predictions of the prophets agree, as it is written, After this I will come back, and will rebuild the house of David, which has fallen; I will rebuild its [very] ruins, and I will set it up again, so that the rest of men may seek the Lord, and all the Gentiles upon whom My name has been invoked.*

The point is, we must separate what the Word of God says from our man-made church laws, regulations, and traditions. Jesus addressed this very issue when He confronted the Pharisees.

> *And He said unto them, Full well ye reject the commandment of God, that ye may keep your own tradition* (Mark 7:9).

What a powerful statement that is indeed! How much priority have we given our man-made laws and traditions over the instructions of God's Word? In how many areas of worship have we limited God by choosing for ourselves what we considered proper and respectable behavior for our church setting? If we, as the Body of Christ worldwide, were to honestly compare the order and traditions of our weekly church services against the expressed desires and commandments of God, a vast number of us would have to admit that we have rejected the commandments of God in order to keep our own traditions.

A true worshiper will embrace the truth of God's Word over man's tradition in every area. God's Word is the highest and final authority. We honor and revere God as holy when we allow our minds to be transformed to His desire and will. In Matthew chapter 15, Jesus deals directly with the issue of man's doctrinal traditions versus the commandment of God. He teaches that our tradition not only makes the commandment of God *"of none effect,"* but that the worship of these man-made doctrines over His Word is in vain. The power of man's traditions have been one of God's greatest enemies. May we learn to surrender ourselves to the desire of God's will so that our worship may not be in vain.

> *Why do ye also transgress the commandment of God by your tradition? …Thus have ye made the commandment of God of none effect by your tradition. …But in vain they do worship Me, teaching for doctrines the commandments of men* (Matthew 15:3b,6,9).

What then is God's holy commandment regarding the dance? It declares, *"Let them praise His name in the dance"* (Ps. 149:3a). Therefore, the Lord's warning to Peter applies to us as well.

…What God has cleansed and pronounced clean, do not you defile and profane by regarding and calling common and un-hallowed or unclean (Acts 10:15 AMP).

Third, if Peter had decided to play it safe and not step out in preaching to the Gentiles, he would have hindered the work of the Lord. Just as Peter put God's will first in spite of inevitable opposition from the other apostles, so the Church must begin to step out to restore the dance in spite of the opposition that will arise when obedience to God stands in contrast to man's traditions. God's timing is always perfect, and He has designated a time for each individual congregation to begin this restoration. We must be sensitive to the leading of God, for the restoration must not be forced at the wrong time any more than it should be denied at the right time.

Fourth, when Peter broke tradition by undertaking the unheard-of task of preaching the gospel to the Gentiles, God affirmed his obedience with a demonstration of spirit and power—the Gentiles received the baptism of the Holy Spirit and spoke in tongues. My personal experience in the dance parallels this example as well. For I have stepped out in obedience to God many times, knowing full well that there were people in attendance who were skeptical or obviously opposed to dance. Likewise, many pastors, knowing there would be at least a measure of opposition from the congregation, have stepped out in faith and obedience to God by inviting my dance company to their churches. God has wondrously met us in our obedience just as He met Peter that day. So far, we have never danced without God granting a manifestation of His grace through the demonstration of His Spirit and power, showing His stamp of approval of our worship.

I will be the first to admit that opposition and the introduction of something new go hand-in-hand. Yet we must ask ourselves: Who do we fear and desire to please, man or God? What do we obey, God's Word or the traditions of men?

God's Word instructs us to praise His name in the dance. We also know that He is *the same yesterday, today, and forever*" (see Heb. 13:8).

Therefore, let us renew our minds according to His Word, not defiling or profaning this gift of dance by following man's tradition of calling it common, unhallowed, or unclean. Let us seek to apply God's truth concerning dance in our churches, giving heed to the Word of God in a way that honors Him and reflects His original purpose for this gift.

CHAPTER 3

〜

Original Purpose

Back in 1986, a particular incident took place that inspired me to write this chapter. The incident I speak of revealed that not only was there a need for those in the Church to understand God's original purpose for creating the dance, but that there are those who struggle with the fact that God created it at all.

An old, traditional view that dance is evil and a work of the devil has caused many to reason that God would not create such a thing. It had never occurred to me before that anyone would think dance had not been created by God until one day, in sharing with my daughter's teacher, a sweet Baptist minister's wife, I quickly became aware of this way of thinking.

I had been invited to the Baptist school to teach some basic sign language to my daughter's kindergarten class. I decided to use a simple Christian song to aid in the learning. The teacher agreed that would be nice. When I happened to mention how beautiful and worshipful it is to sign to a worship song, I quickly found myself disinvited and was told that they could not allow such a thing.

In my confusion, I questioned this sudden reaction and found the root of the problem. Sign language, as a rhythmic movement expressed to music, was too closely related to dance, and this teacher believed that dance in any form was carnal and evil. As our conversation continued, I was most surprised to find that this dedicated Christian woman firmly believed that dance had not been created by God. Not only did she view it as evil, but she also felt it had been completely fabricated by the devil.

Satan is no creator; he is only out to pervert and steal God's creation. That day I realized that the deception surrounding the dance had roots that grew much deeper than I had ever anticipated. I also realized that satan must be completely exposed for the counterfeit thief and liar that he really is.

> *All things were made and came into existence through Him; and without Him was not even one thing made that has come into being* (John 1:3 AMP).

> *For from Him and through Him and to Him are all things. [For all things originate with Him and come from Him...]* (Romans 11:36a AMP).

The Scriptures clearly spell out that all things originate with God and that nothing has come into being apart from Him. These Scripture references repeatedly use the term *all things*, which include the dance. You may ask, "Are you saying that God created things like secular music, drugs, immoral sex, and so on? Because these things exist, and they must have originated somewhere." Secular music, drugs, and immoral sex are only perversions of gifts that are good and perfect according to God's original intention. God created music for praise and worship to His glory. Drugs are derived from plants and herbs, which were created with medicinal purposes for health and healing. Sex was created for reproduction and the intimate holy union between a man and wife. Our most valuable gifts have been the target of satan's greatest perversions.

If God created the dance, then what was His original intent and purpose? The attempt to answer this question is a tall order. It would be presumptuous of me to even begin to assume that I fully understand God's original plan and purpose for the dance in its entirety. But I am thankful for the hidden treasures of truth that God has generously revealed to me thus far.

The unfolding of these truths is a progressive process. If we skipped right to the meat of this matter, there would surely be those who would spit it out or, at best, choke on it in rejection, unable to digest it in its strongest form. We can't eat meat if we haven't even tasted milk. In this chapter, the answer to this question will be more in line with the milk of the matter, although this book in its entirety will definitely introduce a healthy portion of meat as well.

The dance, as we have known it in the world, has been functioning in an area outside of its original purpose. Therefore, its true value has been drastically misunderstood, damaged, and even lost. We cannot hope to see the orderly restoration of dance until we understand the basic function God originally intended it to accomplish.

Let's look at a natural example of this principle: If you owned a Phillips-head screwdriver and had no idea as to its original purpose, you might attempt to use it in any number of ways, such as to prop open a window or to stir a can of paint, but without understanding the actual purpose for its design and creation, you would never fully appreciate the value of that tool. (If you've ever tried to unscrew a Phillips-head screw with anything other than a Phillips-head screwdriver, you will understand the value of using this tool in the function for which it was created.) The Phillips-head screwdriver and the Phillips-head screw were specifically made for one another and work together to fulfill the purpose for which they were originally and jointly created.

The dance and man were also specifically created for one another. They are also to work together to fulfill the purpose for which each was created. Unfortunately, many have yet to understand God's basic purpose for creating man, much less His purpose for the dance. If we lack understanding as to why God created man in the first place, then we're certainly not going to understand, or probably even care, why He created dance. In reality, God's overall basic purpose for the dance is no different than it is for His creation not only of man, but of all things.

Purpose and Pleasure

*Thou art worthy, O Lord, to receive glory and honour and power: for Thou hast created **all things**, and for Thy **pleasure** they are and were created* (Revelation 4:11).

This Scripture proclaims quite clearly that God's purpose for the creation of all things is His pleasure. Thus, we can safely say that His purpose is His pleasure, and His pleasure is His purpose.

In direct connection to this we find in Psalm 149:3-4 that God's Word says, *"Let them praise His name in the dance"* (Ps. 149:3a). The very next verse says, *"For the Lord taketh **pleasure** in His people"* (Ps. 149:4a). This word, *pleasure*, is a Hebrew word, which means "to be pleased with, to satisfy, be acceptable, set affections on, approve of, delight in, enjoy, and a favorable thing." God not only favorably accepts and approves of the dance, He also sets His affections on it, finding satisfaction, enjoyment, and delight in it.

To support this point, let's examine the Greek and Hebrew word definitions for the words *purpose* and *pleasure*, in order to further prove that His purpose is His pleasure and His pleasure is His purpose. Ecclesiastes 3:1 tells us that there is a time for every *purpose* under the heaven. The word *purpose*, is the Hebrew word *chephets*, and it is almost identical in meaning to the Greek word *thelema*, meaning *pleasure*, which can be found in our previous Scripture of Revelation 4:11. *Chephets* (purpose) is defined as pleasure, purpose, desire, delight, acceptable, a valuable thing; while *thelema* (pleasure) is defined as purpose, pleasure, desire, determination, choice, inclination, will.

Putting these definitions together, along with the other Scriptures that we have examined, we can say, "The inclination and determination of God's heart was to create the dance. It was His choice and purpose to make it an acceptable, enjoyable, valuable, delightful thing, fulfilling His desire with the purpose of bringing Him pleasure according to His will."

Fulfilling God's Purpose

To some, it may seem almost silly that such basic truths would have to be addressed, but even the simplest of truths have been robbed from the understanding of the Church, and without them we would not have a leg to stand on or a foundation to build upon. The enemy knows that without the *truth* man will never *be free*. Scripture tells us that it is the *truth* that *sets us free* (see John 8:32). And it also tells us that Jesus Christ is the truth (see John 14:6). Therefore, we will never be free without Jesus. No wonder He is called the Cornerstone (see Ps. 118:22 NASB), for *truth* and *freedom* are definitely foundational issues.

It is the purpose and pleasure of God's heart for man to come to know the freedom, life, and salvation provided for him through the sacrifice of God's Son, Jesus Christ, on the Cross. If we never come to the understanding of the purpose for the life, death, and resurrection of Jesus Christ, we will never truly understand the purpose for our life on this earth, much less the purpose for the dance. God created all things, including the dance, to work together for the good to those who love Him and are called according to His purpose (see Rom. 8:28).

What, then, is the purpose to which God has called us and what role could the dance possibly play in accomplishing it? Scripture states that we have been called to conform to the image of Christ (see Rom. 8:29). As we examine this, we see two basic purposes for which Christ came. The first is found in Luke 19:10, *"For the Son of man is come to seek and to save that which was lost."* The second is found in First John 3:8b (AMP), *"The reason the Son of God was made manifest (visible) was to undo (destroy, loosen, and dissolve) the works the devil [has done]."*

Remembering that all things work together for the good, let's begin by examining the first purpose as it relates to the dance. If Christ came to seek and save that which was lost, how does dance help to accomplish this foundational purpose? Let's return to Psalm 149:3-4, the dance Scripture we examined previously. In studying these verses, we have already discovered the basic truth that the Lord takes pleasure in His people when they praise Him in the dance. If we continue to read these verses, we will begin to see the connection between the demonstration of dance and God's salvation: *"For the Lord takes pleasure in His people; He will beautify the afflicted ones with salvation"* (Ps. 149:4 NASB).

In my testimony at the beginning of this book, I explained that I had decided to lay down dance entirely due to the fact that I could not understand how it had anything whatsoever to do with serving God, bringing salvation to others, or glorifying Him in any way. That was simply a lack of knowledge according to God's Word. For the Scripture says when we praise the Lord in the dance, He takes pleasure in it and He will beautify the afflicted ones with salvation. Not only have I witnessed the demonstration of the dance bringing salvation to those who had not previously known Christ, but I have also seen how it breathes a new hope and inspiration into the afflicted, saving them from spiritual strongholds that possess them and hold them captive.

This brings us to, and beautifully connects us with, the second purpose of Christ in the earth: *"The reason the Son of God was made manifest, (visible) was to undo (destroy, loosen, and dissolve) the works the devil [has done]"* (1 John 3:8b AMP). Not only does the dance set the captives free, undoing, destroying, loosening, and dissolving the works of the enemy, it also binds the enemy with chains and fetters of iron, executing God's judgment upon him (see Ps. 149:7-9; see also Chapter 10, Spiritual Warfare and the Dance).

Although these functions of the dance are basic and foundational, they are not recognized or understood by the majority of people in the Church today. Dance was created to be a functioning, powerful tool of communication in the Kingdom of God to His glory. Dance is a two-edged sword in the hands of the believer as it administers and imparts God's Word; it possesses the same power and effects of that Word; and it conveys the power of that Word to bring salvation to the afflicted and freedom to those who were bound. It was created to help accomplish this purpose of God in the earth. Satan wants to stop this type of work in any form. Satan's works represent and produce bondage and death, while the works of Christ represent and produce freedom and salvation unto eternal life.

Victory, Restoration, and Celebration

Throughout the Scripture, the dance is strongly linked to life, freedom, salvation, restoration, and victory over the enemy. The very first biblical account that uses the word *dance* is in reference to Miriam, when she picked up her tambourine and led her people in a victory dance after they were safely delivered across the Red Sea. Pharaoh's approaching army would have brought certain death, but God brought salvation, freedom, victory, and life—the response to which was appropriately expressed through the demonstration of dance (see Exod. 15:20). The very last biblical account that uses the word *dance* is in reference to the return of the prodigal son. The joy of his repentance and reunion with the father was appropriately expressed by celebration, music, and dancing in the father's house (see Luke 15:25). Therefore, we see dance is strongly connected with salvation, freedom, victory, life, and restoration.

Throughout Jeremiah chapters 30 and 31 the message of God's salvation, restoration, and victory over the enemy are clearly and boldly proclaimed. It is no coincidence that the dance is so tightly interwoven in these Scriptures, for God has created it as a type, symbol, and appropriate expression of victory, praise, and thanksgiving.

> *"For, behold, days are coming," declares the Lord, "when I will restore the fortunes of My people Israel and Judah." The Lord says, "I will also bring them back to the land that I gave to their forefathers, and they shall possess it. ...And it shall come*

about on that day," declares the Lord of hosts, "that I will break his yoke from off their neck, and will tear off their bonds; and strangers shall no longer make them their slaves. …Therefore all who devour you shall be devoured; and all your adversaries, every one of them, shall go into captivity; and those who plunder you shall be for plunder, and all who prey upon you I will give for prey. For I will restore you to health and I will heal you of your wounds," declares the Lord, "Because they have called you an outcast, saying: 'It is Zion; no one cares for her.'" Thus says the Lord, "Behold, I will re-store the fortunes of the tents of Jacob and have compassion on his dwelling places; and the city shall be rebuilt on its ruin, and the palace shall stand on its rightful place. And from them shall proceed thanksgiving and the voice of those who make merry [dance]…*"* (Jeremiah 30:3,8,16-19 NASB).

"Again I will build you, and you shall be rebuilt, O virgin of Israel! Again you shall take up your tambourines, and go forth to the dances of the merrymakers." …For the Lord has ran-somed Jacob, and redeemed him from the hand of him who was stronger than he, and they shall come and shout for joy on the height of Zion…. "Then the virgin shall rejoice in the dance, and the young men and the old, together, for I will turn their mourning into joy, and will comfort them, and give them joy for their sorrow" (Jeremiah 31:4,11-13 NASB).

Salvation, breaking yokes, tearing off bonds, freedom from slavery, and victory over the enemy, along with restoration, healing, and re-building of ruins are all appropriately connected with tambourines, shouts for joy, thanksgiving, and dancing. In these scriptural exam-ples, we see the dance being expressed after the fact in response to the victory that they had already received.

As New Testament worshipers, we can also appropriately celebrate the victory in praise and thanksgiving through the dance. The differ-ence between Old Testament dancers and New Testament dancers is that we have the assurance of our victory over the enemy in advance, due to the precious work of the Cross of Jesus Christ.

Truth Restored

It is vitally important that these truths and their fundamental functions be restored to the Church. Without an understanding of these simple truths, we will have nothing solid to build upon in the restoration of dance. For it is the truth that holds us up and gives us the ability to stand against the enemy's lies. Truth itself is an important part of the whole armor of God.

> *Wherefore take unto you the whole armour of God, that ye may be able to withstand in the evil day, and having done all, to stand. Stand therefore, having your loins girt about with truth...* (Ephesians 6:13-14).

One Greek dictionary describes loins as "procreative power." The physical loins are the area of the lower abdomen between the hips that encompasses the reproductive organs. Spiritually, this represents the area within us that is procreative, having power to produce life. This life-producing area—*our loins*—must be girt about, or encircled and held up by the truth. Now we can begin to understand why satan chooses to attack and rob us of basic, foundational truths. Satan has attacked the spiritual loins of the dance, hoping to annihilate the procreative life-giving power it was created to impart. The Scripture says that our loins must be held up by the truth in order to be able to withstand the enemy. That is why the truth has been such a strategic target for the enemy, and this is why the dance has not been able to stand in the past, much less function in the Church as God originally intended.

Over the years, I have continually witnessed this procreative life-giving power in operation through anointed dance, bringing salvation to the afflicted, while loosening, dissolving, and destroying the works of the devil. On a more personal note, I have also experienced, time after time, the intimacy and honor of gloriously embracing the heart of my God through the abandon of responsive physical expression, encountering a depth of glory, which, to me, has seemed otherwise unattainable.

Yes, God has created all things for His pleasure. His true pleasure is that He will return for a glorious Church without spot or wrinkle, a Bride lacking in nothing—not robbed and deceived, but restored and enlightened. I thank God for this glorious *"period of restoration of all things about which God spoke by the mouth of His holy prophets..."* (Acts 3:21 NASB) back to the original intent and purpose that not only dance, but all things might be restored for the purpose of His glory.

CHAPTER 4

The Roots of Corruption

In light of the glorious truths that we have discovered thus far concerning dance, a few questions may come to mind, such as, what happened to the dance? Why is its God-given purpose not common knowledge? And why isn't the Church fully functioning in it? To satisfactorily answer these questions, we must widen our study to include the origin of worship. For to even begin to understand the purpose of dance, we must seek to understand worship because dance was created for worship. It is a balanced part of God's plan for worship.

Significance of Worship

What is worship? Worship and its significance is the hardest thing I know to try to explain or understand with the carnal mind. Worship is something that existed before the foundation of the earth, exists now, and will continue to exist throughout eternity.

I believe worship to be the most powerful force in the universe. Worship gives great pleasure, honor, and glory to God. It functions as the most personal, intimate, unifying form of communion between man and God. One thing is certain: We the Church have much to understand concerning the power and significance of what actually takes place in the spiritual realm when we worship in spirit and truth.

Being human, we are limited in knowledge as the Scripture says, *"...we see through a glass, darkly... [and] know in part"* (1 Cor. 13:12a). In light of this, I ask that you consider the following passages with the purpose of more fully understanding worship, and God's judgment of anyone seeking its glory for themselves.

Although we yet lack knowledge in these areas, there is one who, to this day, perfectly understands the fullness of the glory and honor that is made manifest through the power of praise and worship. He is one who was highly exalted by God, specifically and perfectly created for the purpose of worship. He was the covering cherub or, in other words, the worship leader in the heavenlies, and his name was lucifer. Lucifer, in Hebrew, is the word *heylel*, which means, "in the sense of brightness, the morning star." His name has its root meaning in the Hebrew word *halel*, meaning "to be clear, to shine, to make a show, to boast, to be clamorously foolish, to rave, to celebrate, commend, glory, give light." This root definition of lucifer's name, *halel*, is translated in the Hebrew as the word *praise, praised, praises, praiseth,* and *praising,* and it is used 102 times throughout the Old Testament. Lucifer's name literally means "to praise." The very definition of his name gives us an idea of the glorious praise that encompasses the throne of God.

Scripture tells us that lucifer was beautiful, anointed, and perfect in his ways from the day he was created. His workmanship encompassed three different categories, which represent all musical instruments as we know them today: *percussion instruments,* represented by tabrets; *wind instruments,* represented by pipes; and stringed instruments, represented by viols.

> *... The workmanship of thy tabrets [percussion] and of thy pipes [wind] was prepared in thee in the day that thou wast created. Thou art the anointed cherub that covereth; and I have set thee so: thou wast upon the holy mountain of God;*

thou hast walked up and down in the midst of the stones of fire. Thou wast perfect in thy ways from the day thou wast created, till iniquity was found in thee (Ezekiel 28:13-15).

But because of the great glory, honor, and power that was entrusted to lucifer, he became proud in his anointing and wanted to exalt himself above God. God could not tolerate this rebellion, and lucifer was cast out of the heavens.

Thy pomp is brought down to the grave, and the noise of thy viols [stringed instruments]: the worm is spread under thee, and the worms cover thee. How art thou fallen from heaven, O Lucifer, son of the morning! how art thou cut down to the ground, which didst weaken the nations! For thou hast said in thine heart, I will ascend into heaven, I will exalt my throne above the stars of God: I will sit also upon the mount of the congregation, in the sides of the north: I will ascend above the height of the clouds; I will be like the most High (Isaiah 14:11-14).

Thine heart was lifted up because of thy beauty, thou hast corrupted thy wisdom by reason of thy brightness: I will cast thee to the ground... (Ezekiel 28:17).

When lucifer was cast out of the heavens, he received a name change from God. It was a humiliating demotion. Once *lucifer*, entrusted with all the beauty that name represented, God now addressed him as *satan*, meaning opponent, arch-enemy, adversary, the accuser, the devil, and he was cast out.

I beheld Satan as lightning fall from heaven (Luke 10:18b).

In order to understand the connection between these events and the damaging effects they eventually had on the dance, as well as upon all worship, we must dig deeper and examine the basic characteristics of this lucifer/satan being. The motivation for lucifer's corruption is revealed in the Scriptures. These Scriptures can help us begin to understand how he operates and the motivations behind his actions that continue to this day.

We see in Scripture that the pride and jealousy of satan that led him to betray God are directly connected to one key concept—satan coveted God's glory. However, God will not give His glory to another; He prizes it as His own name (see Isa. 42:8,11). Therefore, let's take a moment to more closely examine the word *glory*.

Glory

Glory is another concept that is difficult to explain or understand with the carnal mind. It is better understood with the spirit. God, in all His majesty, is glorious, and it is only through personally experiencing the presence of God that we can ever even begin to understand the great wonder of His glory.

In Scripture the word *glory* is used to describe God's manifest presence. He alone is glorious and worthy to receive glory. I'd like to make a distinction between God's glory and His being glorified in worship. As I've already said, the word *glory* best describes the manifest presence of God, and this kind of glory does not depend upon our praise and worship or even upon our existence. The thing that truly amazes me is that God has given man the honor and ability to give Him glory and even manifest His glory by using our God-given gifts to magnify who He is.

This is where the character of lucifer becomes relevant. The beauty, brightness, and wisdom lucifer possessed was a gift created within him for the purpose of giving glory to God, but lucifer chose to use his gift to magnify and glorify himself. This self-seeking glory is the foundation of satan's nature, reflecting all that he does in the earth today.

Merchandising the Glory

As I studied the scriptural accounts concerning lucifer's fall, I found something I hadn't seen before dealing with the reason why he was cast down.

By the multitude of thy merchandise they have filled the midst of thee with violence, and thou hast sinned: therefore I will cast thee as profane out of the mountain of God: and I will destroy thee, O covering cherub, from the midst of the stones of fire. …Thou has defiled thy sanctuaries by the multitude of thine iniquities, by the iniquity of thy traffick… (Ezekiel 28:16,18).

These two key words, *merchandise* and *traffick* have the same reference number (#7404) in James Strong's Concordance, indicating merchandising and trade as a peddler. The basic meaning of the word *merchandise* is to buy and sell, to promote the sale of a product.

What could it have been that lucifer was buying and selling? What product could he possibly have been promoting? The product he promoted was himself. And what gave his sales technique such power? It was his God-given ability to glorify through his beauty, wisdom, brightness, and his anointing to excel in these areas. And what did he attempt to gain for himself through the power of these God-given gifts? The worship of the angels, which belonged to God. Plain and simple, lucifer betrayed God by merchandising what was meant exclusively for the glory of God.

Lucifer was perfectly created for worship and was himself an instrument through which glory was manifested. He attempted to keep the profits of glory, honor, and power for himself. This was the beginning of evil as satan gave birth to the greatest deception and most hideous abomination that is now common to man—the merchandising of what exclusively belongs to God for His glory. We all, like lucifer, were perfectly created for God's glory in the wide variety of gifts and talents that were prepared in us from the day when we were created. Yes, man was created for the glory of God.

*…Bring My sons from far, and My daughters from the ends of the earth; even every one that is called by My name: **for I have created him for My glory**…* (Isaiah 43:6-7).

Yet, as we have seen, God clearly states, *"My glory will I not give to another"* (Isa. 42:8). Since we have all been given something of value with which to worship God, we must understand the deceptive sin in keeping any profits of glory for ourselves. This sin of merchandising not only robs God, but as we are about to see, it results in the defiling of God's holy temple.

Defiling the Temple

God's word to lucifer was, *"Thou hast defiled thy sanctuaries by the multitude of thine iniquities, by the iniquity of thy traffick..."* (Ezek. 28:18). Ezekiel 28:16 recounts God's reaction to this merchandising and trafficking:

> *By the multitude of thy merchandise they have filled the midst of thee with violence, and thou hast sinned: **therefore I will cast thee as profane out of the mountain of God: and I will destroy thee...*** (Ezekiel 28:16).

Looking to the New Testament, we see that God has not changed in His reaction to the defiling of His holy temple.

> *Know ye not that ye are the temple of God, and that the Spirit of God dwelleth in you? If any man defile the temple of God, him shall God destroy; for the temple of God is holy, which temple ye are* (1 Corinthians 3:16-17).

Our minds must be transformed and renewed to the original purpose of God's creation for man. God placed gifts within us so that He would be glorified in and through us and that we would commune, have love for, and become one with Him and one another. However, many men have followed in the footsteps of lucifer, who as satan, has deceived them due to a lack of knowledge of the truth. This has resulted in the common practice of merchandising to the glory and profit of man, thereby robbing God of what rightfully belongs to Him. This sheds a whole new light on this New Testament passage:

And the Jews' passover was at hand, and Jesus went up to Jerusalem, and found in the temple those that sold oxen and sheep and doves, and the changers of money sitting: and when He had made a scourge of small cords, He drove them all out of the temple, and the sheep, and the oxen; and poured out the changers' money, and overthrew the tables; and said unto them that sold doves, Take these things hence; make not My Father's house an house of merchandise (John 2:13-16).

The first time I read this Scripture, I was surprised that Jesus lost His temper, overturned tables, and emptied out their money, while hurling a whip at man and beast. However, I now see that His righteous anger went much deeper than this one isolated incident. It represented the entire series of abominations that first began with the merchandising of lucifer in the heavenlies.

Relating this same incident, Matthew records these words of Jesus in his Gospel, *"...My house shall be called the house of prayer; but ye have made it a **den of thieves**"* (Matt. 21:13). Regardless of the reason—lack of knowledge or any other—merchandising of that which was exclusively created for the glory of God, including every gift and talent bestowed on man, robs God of what is rightfully His. All those who do so are considered thieves in the eyes of God.

God cries out over the defilement of His gifts and His temple: *"O ye sons of men, how long will you turn My glory into shame? how long will ye love vanity, and seek after leasing?"* (Ps. 4:2).

How does this merchandising of the glory and defiling of God's temple relate to dance? We have already established through Scripture that dance is an instrument of glory, a powerful tool of communication, which accomplishes the pleasure and purpose of God. Unfortunately, satan has twisted these characteristics to his own purpose and pleasure, while communicating a perverted message of darkness. Because of the God-given power of dance to clearly communicate, man, as well as satan, has taken this holy gift and shamefully merchandised with it.

One afternoon I decided to leave the TV on in the living room to conduct a little survey of my own. I wanted to see the variety of ways in which dance was used to merchandise the products of men. Every time I heard a commercial come on, I checked to see if it used dance in any fashion. In one afternoon, I witnessed dance being used to sell milk, gum, candy bars, fast foods, fabric softener, cheese, airline tickets, shoes, several different soft drinks, and blue jeans. Before God began to reveal His truth to me concerning His purpose for dance, I would have thought nothing of using my gift of dance to promote soft drinks or fast foods in a commercial. But the Spirit of God has convicted me that dance is a holy thing and that it was created specifically for the worship, glory, honor, and power of God. Therefore, I have personally chosen to reserve dance in my life exclusively for God.

Since I have chosen to exclusively serve God with the dance, am I automatically free from the sin of merchandising with this gift? By no means! We must not allow ourselves to be fooled. If a Christian dancer is motivated by the desire for recognition and praise from fellow Christians as a beautiful, anointed dancer, then that dancer is no different than lucifer who wanted the glory for his God-given gifts and beauty.

Although the fact that the dance was created to glorify God is a basic, fundamental truth, the enemy has desperately worked out a strategy throughout the ages to disguise even the most foundational purpose of it from the Church. As human beings we have but one lifetime to learn and overcome these strategies, but we must realize that the enemy with which we contend is an ancient being—one who has subtly been working his plan of deception into the understanding of the Church throughout many generations. Our only defense against the wisdom of this ancient strategic plan is to be found in the Word of God.

Lucifer was given by God, and still possesses to this day, wisdom and understanding of worship and its power and significance that far exceeds our understanding. When lucifer fell, he did not lose his wisdom, it merely became corrupt: "*...thou has corrupted thy wisdom* *by reason of thy brightness…"* (Ezek. 28:17). We must understand that with this very wisdom, he has succeeded in the rape, retardation, and perversion of man's fuller understanding and growth in worship to our God.

It is true that the Church has not understood the full significance of what takes place in the spiritual realm when we worship. Although worship is not as much about understanding as doing, I believe that we are greatly limited by our lack of knowledge.

The good news is that God's Word promises us that in the last days our knowledge will be increased (see Dan. 12:4), and many truths that have been hidden will be revealed and restored. Just as God is the creator of all things, He is also the restorer of all things. And I thank God that dance is being restored to take its rightful place as a balanced part of God's overall plan for worship.

CHAPTER 5

~

Dance in the World

One day during a regular visit, my dentist casually asked me what kind of dance I taught. As I briefly shared my call with him, he asked, "What is the difference between Christian dance and worldly dance?"

Worldly dance does not reflect God's character, and it is a perversion of God's original purpose for creating it. Noah Webster's dictionary tells us that the word *perversion* comes from the Latin word *perverto*, meaning to turn from truth, propriety, or from proper purpose; to distort from true use or end; as to pervert reason by misdirecting; to pervert the laws by misinterpreting and misapplying. I'm not saying that all secular dance is intentionally bad or evil, but I am saying that because of our lack of understanding, dance has been misinterpreted, misapplied, distorted, and turned from its proper purpose.

Worldly dance may very well be perverted by God's standard, but dance in itself is not perverted. Dance itself is something that we call amoral, meaning it has no morals of its own. Dance was created as an effective, powerful tool of communication and its moral or immoral value depends upon how it is used. Jesus said, *"He who is not with Me [definitely on My side] is against Me, and he who does not [definitely] gather with Me and for My side scatters"* (Matt. 12:30 AMP).

The black and white truth in these words of Jesus will help us to rightly divide and clearly judge whether the function of any particular dance is godly or ungodly, moral or immoral. It's as simple as that. We're either definitely on His side or we're against Him; we're either part of the gathering process, or we are part of the scattering. *Gather* is the Greek word *sunago*—*sun*, meaning union, and *ago*, meaning to lead. Thus, "to lead to union" sums up the function of godly dance, which is to lead to union with Christ. *Scatter*, on the other hand, is the Greek word *skorpizo*, meaning the idea of penetrating, to dissipate, waste. This word *skorpizo* is where we get our word *scorpion*, which we all know refers to a creature with a poisonous, deadly sting. If a dance does not gather by imparting life and leading to union with Christ, it falls into the category of scattering by penetrating, dissipating, and creating waste. Several definitions of waste are empty, to accomplish nothing, to be used inefficiently, not productive, worthless, that in which no value is found.

Any one of these terms is descriptive of dance that does not fulfill God's original purpose for creating it. As beautiful and skillful as some secular forms of dance may seem, in relation to God's Kingdom they are empty, non-productive, non-efficient, worthless, and of no true value. According to God's Word there is no in-between; you are either hot or cold for Him or against Him—being lukewarm is not acceptable.

> *I know thy works, that thou art neither cold nor hot: I would thou wert cold or hot. So then because thou art lukewarm, and neither cold nor hot, I will spue thee out of My mouth* (Revelation 3:15-16).

I know that some of these definitions may sound extreme at first, but we must not underestimate the spiritual power of the communication and persuasion of emotions that are characteristics of dance. These God-given effects were originally intended for the purpose of gathering unto His glory, but in the hands of the enemy, these characteristics are equally as effective in expressing communication and persuasion that scatters from Christ and gathers unto the kingdom of this world.

Power to Persuade—For Good or Evil

One story that comes to mind that illustrates the deadly penetrating effects of ungodly dance is found in the Gospel of Mark. It is the story of Herod and the daughter of Herodias.

> But an opportune time came [for Herodias] when Herod on his birthday gave a banquet for his nobles and the high military commanders and chief men of Galilee. For when the daughter of Herodias herself came in and danced, she pleased and fascinated Herod and his guests; and the king said to the girl, Ask me for whatever you desire, and I will give it to you. And he put himself under oath to her, Whatever you ask me, I will give it to you, even to the half of my kingdom (Mark 6:21-23 AMP).

That must have been some persuasive dance to cause a king to voluntarily put himself under oath to a girl in front of his nobles, all those high military officials, and the chief men of Galilee. In front of all these witnesses, he vowed to give her whatever she would desire up to *half of his kingdom*. What could possibly have caused Herod to give such an extreme response? Well, Scripture says that her *dance "pleased and fascinated"* him. The word *pleased* is the Greek word *aresko*, meaning "to excite the emotions."

We can only speculate as to the precise type of dance that the girl did, but from Herod's response, we can see that it was definitely not a godly dance; its effects were, without question, not only damaging but deadly. Due to her mother's promptings, the girl asked for the head of John the Baptist on a platter. And even though the girl's request grieved the king, it was granted.

This dance did not, in any way, gather or lead to Christ and His Kingdom. Instead, the piercing, intoxicating effect of that girl's dance scattered, or *skorpizo*, through its penetrating, poisonous persuasion. And death to John the Baptist was the end result.

Dancers beware, for dance was created with the power to excite the emotions of man. Emotions are a powerful part of a man's soul, and the door to a man's soul is a dangerous one to open if the influence you bring is not one of godliness.

Dance is a mysterious and glorious gift, full of untapped spiritual treasures. Birthed from the Father's heart, dance has been fashioned for a purpose yet to be discovered by most. Dance, as we have known it, is a beautiful art form that can pierce the heart, convict, and convince, either for good or evil.

Dance definitely has a mysterious, spiritual power that affects man deeply and, by nature, spontaneously brings some form of surrender. One short dance can change the course of a life, for it has a power that directly connects the audience with a high-voltage communication line to whatever it is that the dancer is communicating. As Herodias' daughter danced for Herod, he was apparently captivated, entranced, and overpowered to the point of willfully submitting and relinquishing the treasures of his life and kingdom into the hands of this girl.

Nothing can cause a man to fall quicker than a suggestive, seductive, alluring dance. This type of persuasion and temptation reminds me of a Yogi Bear cartoon that I saw as a child.

Yogi Bear has always had a weakness for blueberry pie. One day, as he was innocently about his business in the woods, a woman in a nearby cabin placed a freshly baked blueberry pie on the windowsill to cool. As the aroma drifted through the air, finding its way directly to Yogi, he became entranced, captivated, and helplessly overtaken. He literally began to float through the air, as the visible aroma formed the shape of a hand that was motioning and luring him in. Boo Boo, his little friend, walked alongside like a little conscience, warning him that this would lead to trouble. Boo Boo reminded him that Ranger Smith would not be a happy camper, but Yogi acted as though he could not hear him as the seductive power of the aroma led him around.

Unfortunately, when he reached his destination, reality struck as the woman screamed, "Help! A bear!" and repeatedly beat him over his dusty head with a broom.

This same type of mysteriously alluring, seductive power operates in worldly dance, causing godly men to run from it and godly women to despise it. Dance is a spiritually powerful force, but it was created that way for a pure and holy purpose.

One of the reasons that dance affects the nature of man so power-fully is due to the fact that it is an instinct. Dance is part of the inborn nature of man. When my children were yet too young to walk or even stand alone, they would instinctively bounce to music in sheer delight. *Instinct* is the Latin word *instinguere*, meaning "an inborn tendency to behave in a way characteristic of a species." I don't see my dog tap-ping her paw to music, for it is not characteristic of her species.

We are of the species of man. Scripture tells us that man was cre-ated in the image of God. If dance is an inborn instinct of man, and man was created in the image of God, does this mean that God also dances? Scripture tells us that He does indeed.

> *The Lord thy God in the midst of thee is mighty; He will save, He will rejoice over thee with joy; He will rest in His love, He will joy over thee with singing* (Zephaniah 3:17).

This word *joy* is the Hebrew word *gool*, meaning "to spin around under the influence of any violent emotion." Noah Webster's dictionary tells us that *violent* means "forcible, moving or acting with physical strength." Our God is mighty in the midst of us as He not only sings over us, but spins around, moving forcibly and acting with physical strength under the influence of great and powerful emotion in His love for us. This is our biblical example of the dance of God. For man to re-spond in such a fashion is nothing more than an inborn tendency to be-have in a way that is characteristic of our Father.

Remembering that the dance will either gather or scatter, consider this: In Zephaniah 3:18, directly after the dance of the Lord is demonstrated, God says, *"I will **gather** them that are sorrowful for the solemn assembly…"* (Zeph. 3:18). The next two verses state, *"…I will save her that halteth, and **gather** her that was driven out…At that time will I bring you again, even in the time that I **gather** you…"* (Zeph. 3:19-20).

The Lord Himself demonstrates the power of godly dance, and the three verses that follow this demonstration boldly declare, "I will gather. I will gather. I will gather." This passage is an exciting revelation for the ministry of dance; it clearly reflects the God-given function and power of the dance to *sunago*, or gather unto the Lord.

Pitfalls of Worldly Dance

It is no coincidence that words like *rejoice and joy* are used to define the dance. For the dance was created as a joyful, pleasurable experience. By nature man loves to dance, and there are many pitfalls of which Christians must beware. These pitfalls are worldly, and due to a lack of knowledge, they have, unfortunately, been widely accepted by many in the Christian community. I would like to take the time to share some of the pitfalls concerning worldly dance. In sharing these pitfalls, I must confess that I both participated in and taught some of these styles of dance for many years before God revealed His purpose for dance to me and renewed my mind.

As we look to the theatrical entertainment facet of dance, we see that it covers a wide variety of forms from children's dance recitals to musicals, ballets, TV variety shows, night clubs, and even the more seductive, perverse forms of so-called adult entertainment. Then we have the less formal forms of dance, such as is expressed by the average American who loves to dance just for the fun of it. This type of dancing would include that which is done in bars and clubs, at weddings, etc.

Although some of these dance forms may seem quite harmless, the perversity of seductive suggestion has filtered its way into even the most innocent of these secular forms. Consider children's dance recitals. Little ones as young as four and five years of age have been taught to shake their pelvises, bat their eyelashes, and throw kisses to an audience that goes wild, clapping, whistling, and calling it cute. Many costumes are designed with feathers, fringes, sequins, and lace, which accentuate breasts, hips, and buttocks. Some are low cut in the top while leaving legs and midriffs exposed. Mesh hose, garters, and long gloves are often added to complete the picture, causing innocent children to look like dance hall girls. What are we doing to our children?

Because of my past occupation of teaching dance in the world, I still receive stacks of costume catalogues in the mail every year. These catalogues are designed especially for children's dance recitals and are sent free of charge to practically every dance studio in America. Just to give you an idea of the spirit behind many of these costumes, I have written down some names of the costumes as they are labeled in the catalogues for ordering.

Any one of these names would be fitting for the billboard of your local X-rated movie theater: Dirty Dinah, Big and Easy, Prove Your Love, Rev It Up, Passion, Ooh La La, Bad, Let It Loose, Show Your Stuff, Close Contact, Wild Thing, Kiss of Fire, Night Moves, After Six, Some Like It Hot, Power of Persuasion, Material Girl, Born to Be Wild, Walk on the Wild Side, Dangerous Curves, Bewitched, Hot and Spicy, Casino, Black Magic, Wild Side, Hot Stuff, Wild Life, Too Hot, Whoopee, Hot Toddy, Where's the Party, Uptown Girl, Sophisticated Baby, Fancy Pants, Party Animal, Exposed, and Private Article. This list is only a sample of what many costume catalogues promote, and it seems to get worse every year.

It is hard to believe how deceived and blinded we have become to accept this level of perversity as the norm for our children. Anyone who has attended a dance recital for his or her child, or perhaps the child of a friend or relative, most likely knows exactly what I am talking about. In no way is this an exaggerated picture that I paint. Neither am I trying to point fingers and condemn, but rather, my desire is to expose this deception.

I myself was totally blinded for years by this so-called norm in the world of dance. It wasn't until the Holy Spirit began to reveal my call to dance for the Lord that my eyes slowly opened. Hundreds of thousands of innocent children across our nation attend dancing school each week. Many of these children are from God-fearing, church-going, Christian homes. Sending your child to dance lessons is part of the American dream for many parents and children. But this dream is becoming more like a nightmare in the eyes of a holy God.

If you have a child who continues in dance through high school and wants to go on, it only gets worse. Again, I know because I've been there. The world of dance is highly competitive, self-centered, and full of selfish ambition. For years, I attended dance seminars that lasted six weeks, six days a week, every summer. Dance teachers from major dance companies in New York, Chicago, and Detroit were brought in. It was a grueling six weeks of five to six hours of dance a day. Dancers were left only enough energy to drag themselves home and fall into bed.

The teachers were merciless, and they knew how to dig deep and pull out every ounce of skill the dancers were capable of producing. I remember in one of the modern dance classes, our knees began to bleed through our tights due to a floor movement we were required to do over and over. As a few dancers began to complain, we were basically told, "If you can't stand the heat, get out of the kitchen because this is the real world of dance." Daily instructions were given in advance for those who were going to vomit or pass out. I wondered if six weeks in a Marine boot camp might have made for a more relaxing summer.

With this level of self-sacrifice, the dancer becomes a slave and servant to further development of technique and skill. Dance itself is literally worshiped, and no price is considered too high for those who want to work their way to the top. Your life becomes a sacrifice to a god called dance. I was sucked in and seduced by the spirit of it all; it is powerful and compelling. At one time, it was so strong that nothing in the world seemed to matter as long as I danced. I personally understand how worldly dance is an idol to the dancer, for it becomes the object of worship and self-sacrificial service as one seeks to move up the ladder.

I'd like to share some revealing comments that I jotted down from a magazine article I read years ago. In this article, some famous ballet dancers, both male and female, were interviewed. In reference to a very famous teacher and choreographer, the dancers said that they knew they were working for the greatest choreographic master of all time. The dancers commented that they knew that the future of their profession depended on whether or how they were noticed by him. The writer of this article commented that in some ways the dancers worshiped the choreographer; in others, they feared him. Always they wanted to please him, and they vied for his attention.

As a dancer in *the* Kingdom of God, I know that I am working for *the* greatest choreographic master of *all* time. I know that my future is not in the hands of a man, but in the hands of God. I worship only Him, fear only Him, and desire to please only Him. Whenever we put any person or thing before God, it is *idolatry.*

> *Their land has also been filled with idols; they worship the work of their hands, that which their fingers have made* (Isaiah 2:8 NASB).

One of the dancers in the interview said, "For some of us ballet is not a profession, it is a religion." Another said, "I never wanted to be anything else. I really don't care what happens to me when I'm through."

I mean no disrespect to these professional dancers; I just believe that they are deceived, and their focus is all wrong. God created dance for worship, not to be worshiped. His purpose is that He would be magnified and glorified in and through it. This is why dance is so powerful, so beautiful, and so precious. However, we were never meant to worship it. It is not the highly developed skill of a dancer that impresses God, but the pure heart of a man who fears and worships Him.

> *He does not delight in the strength of the horse; He does not take pleasure in the legs of a man. The Lord favors those who fear Him...* (Psalm 147:10-11 NASB).

This worship of the dance, the dancer, or even the dance teacher is something that God hates and does not make allowances for in His Word. It is called idol worship. Have you ever wondered why so many persons who have dedicated their lives to dance are homosexuals and lesbians? Man has taken the precious gift of dance, which was created for the glory of God, and exchanged it for glory of self. They have worshiped and idolized the creature and the created rather than the Creator. In Romans chapter 1, we clearly see that homosexuality is a result of these very deeds.

> *And exchanged the glory of the incorruptible God for an image in the form of corruptible man and of birds and four-footed animals and crawling creatures. Therefore God gave them over in the lusts of their hearts to impurity, that their bodies might be dishonored among them. For they exchanged the truth of God for a lie, **and worshiped and served the creature rather than the Creator,** who is blessed forever. Amen. **For this reason** God gave them over to degrading passions; for their women exchanged the natural function for that which is unnatural, and in the same way also the men abandoned the natural function of the woman and burned in their desire toward one another, men with men committing indecent acts and receiving in their own persons the due penalty of their error* (Romans 1:23-27 NASB).

Another aspect of worldly dance is that of *selfish ambition*. In order to be so highly dedicated to the dance itself, a worldly dancer must be highly motivated. I believe that the root of that motivation is the basic need of all men to be accepted and loved. Somewhere along the way, each dancer discovered the gift of dance that he or she was born with. By excelling above the average, these individuals found acceptance and praise from parents, teachers, friends, etc.

The trap is that the more skill you obtain, the more highly esteemed you become in the world of dance; therefore, you receive more love, acceptance, and attention. This keeps the focus of the dancer on skill and obtaining more of it. The spirit behind worldly dance is not only to be a good dancer, but to be the best or better than the others. This breeds an unhealthy environment of competition, jealousy, and selfish ambition. It's a total diversion, perversion, and misapplication of God's original purpose for dance.

> *But if you have bitter jealousy and selfish ambition in your heart, do not be arrogant and so lie against the truth. This wisdom is not that which comes down from above, but is earthly, natural, demonic. For where jealousy and selfish ambition exist, there is disorder and every evil thing* (James 3:14-16 NASB).

This is the fruit that develops as the focus and understanding of the dancer is built on the wrong principles. It is a type of *skorpizo*, a penetrating poisonous sting that scatters, bringing disorder and every evil thing. Scripture says that there is no in-between. You are either one who gathers or one who scatters.

Wholly Dedicated to God

Even as I write this chapter I feel a heavy burden upon my heart for those with a call upon their lives to dance. Therefore, I would like to share one last warning before closing this chapter. If you have stepped out in the revelation of serving the Lord in the dance, you must completely sever your ties with any and every form of worldly dance. You cannot be a gatherer and a scatterer at the same time.

> *You cannot drink the cup of the Lord and the cup of demons; you cannot partake of the table of the Lord and the table of demons* (1 Corinthians 10:21 NASB).

Only one chapter of this book has been dedicated to addressing the basic pitfalls of worldly dance. The fullness of this book is occupied with bringing forth the truth and goodness of this gift. I leave all convicting and convincing to the Holy Spirit. If He brought revelation of truth to me, He can surely bring it to anyone who truly seeks to walk uprightly in his or her call before God. Let us allow Christ and the truth of His Word to be the foundation of our every understanding, and may we truly glorify Him in our hearts, minds, and bodies.

CHAPTER 6

∼

Glorify God in Your Body

Somewhere along the line, the misconception that the believer's physical body is carnal in nature has crept into the Church. Unfortunately, the worship of the Church at large has suffered under this deception. Although this belief is, for the most part, not openly discussed, it projects a negative concept that has directly affected and minimized the fullness of what God desires for worship. If our physical bodies were considered carnal and unacceptable before God, He would not have made them the temple of the Holy Spirit, nor would He have instructed us to glorify Him in them (see 1 Cor. 6:19-20).

Instruments of Service and Worship

Our bodies and the actions we perform with them have, without a doubt, much greater spiritual significance than many Christians realize. The enemy's goal is for us to accept our bodies as carnal, living our lives day by day, consumed with satisfying the appetites and desires of our flesh. God intended the use of our bodies for a much more noble use than this.

He has honored these physical vessels with the deposit of His Holy Spirit. They are acceptable to Him, and He asks that we offer them back to Him for His service.

> *I beseech you therefore, brethren, by the mercies of God, that ye* *present your bodies a living sacrifice, holy, acceptable unto* *God, which is your reasonable service* (Romans 12:1).

In this verse we clearly see the holiness of our bodies in service to the Lord. This word, *service*, is defined in the Greek as "worship." We must understand, then, that what we do with our bodies is considered worship. Because God created us with a free will, the daily movements of our bodies is, therefore, a manifestation of whom we have chosen to worship or serve. Like Joshua, God commands us to *"...choose you this day whom ye will serve"* (Josh. 24:15a). Every day we are faced with many choices of whom we will serve. As we continue to choose God, our lives become a living sacrifice to Him. This is our worshipful service.

Expressions of Love

Every movement that we choose to make throughout the day is a level of spiritual, worshipful service—whether we are cleaning toilets or lying prostrate before the Lord. Each action may, however, express a different level or form of love. For example, throughout the day, I express my love toward my husband on different levels. Things like cleaning the house, cooking meals, and doing laundry are one level of the expression of my love. When my husband comes home, I kiss and hug him. In the evening, we may end up snuggling on the couch as we spend time with our children. These latter forms are more intimate expressions of love than doing his laundry. Yet there are still deeper levels of expression that are reserved for when we are alone and can focus on one another more intimately. The relationship and holy marital union of a man and wife is a beautiful parallel to our worship of God, for we ultimately seek to serve Him and know Him intimately—to consummate our relationship and become one with Him.

The word *consummate* is defined as "complete fulfillment." In both the physical relationship of a husband and wife and the spiritual relationship of man and God, the ultimate goal is the complete fulfillment and satisfaction that is found in unity. You can't get any closer than becoming one. Jesus expressed His desire for oneness with the Father and with us. He said, *"I and My Father are one"* (John 10:30), as well as, *"…ye shall know that I am in My Father, and ye in Me, and I in you"* (John 14:20).

When man and wife become one in spirit by taking the holy vows of matrimony, there is no need for a law that says they must physically consummate their marriage. This expression is a natural response to their love for one another. Wouldn't it be sad if we were taught that man and wife were only to physically unite for the function of necessary reproduction and at no other time? If that were true, we would miss out on a precious gift from God. But as we relate this principle to our worship, we see that many have accepted Him as Lord and Savior; becoming one with Him in spirit without ever experiencing worship at a level any deeper than is necessary to function as part of a congregation for a few minutes on a Sunday morning.

True consummation, complete fulfillment, in your worship is not found in singing a song or performing a gesture such as kneeling, lifting your hands, or dancing. True fulfillment begins with a humbling of heart and the surrendering of all that is within you, which creates a unifying or consummation of spirit between man and God. Singing and gesturing are fulfilling in that they release and express the emotion that is experienced in touching God. Expression without true emotion is empty, and emotion without any form of expression is frustrating, unnatural, and even reflects bondage. It is not frustration, bondage, or emptiness that the Lord seeks in worshipers, but freedom and the complete fulfillment that is found in unity.

The physical outward expressions of our love are beautiful manifestations of our worship, producing a spiritual, holy consummation that was originally created for our fulfillment and satisfaction as well as God's. Dance enables us to enter a level of worship that encompasses all that is within us as we worship, not only in spirit and soul, but also as we respond in adoration through the expression of our physical bodies. There is no clear-cut line describing the limitations of what is or what is not dance. When it comes to the heart being expressed through our physical bodies in our praise and worship, even the gentle swaying of a lifted hand can be a beautiful, pleasing dance before the Lord.

The experience of entering this expressive realm of worship is exciting, yet it can also be painful, for we must battle the strongholds of deep-seated traditions and mind-sets. I shared in the Introduction about the difficult struggle I had concerning the outward expression of any emotion in connection with worship. True worship is definitely an emotional experience, and emotion by nature must be expressed. The word *emotion* itself is derived of two separate words consisting of *out* plus *motion*. Therefore, even the definition of the word *emotion* suggests that our feelings are being expressed in some outward motion, or manifestation.

Verbalizing our love through words and song are the most common and acceptable forms of emotion expressed within the traditional church setting, but we must not stop there. God has made available to us a form of expression that goes beyond thinking or even speaking our love, for we were created by God to act out and express our love. The Greek and Hebrew definitions of the words used for *praise* and *worship* are clearly defined by physical movements and postures such as bowing, kneeling, lifting, clapping, waving of hands, spinning, dancing, leaping, even lying prostrate. These expressions are outward reactions to inward emotions. This is how we glorify our God. It is only natural for man to release in some way what he feels by expressing it in the physical motion of his body.

Rejoice

Rejoicing is another word that accurately describes an outward response to an inward emotion. The word *rejoice*—including *rejoiced, rejoiceth,* and *rejoicing*—is used 283 times in the Bible. This tells me that our rejoicing must be very important to God. Consider the following verses: *"Rejoice in the Lord **always**: and again I say, Rejoice"* (Phil. 4:4); *"In Thy name shall they rejoice **all the day**"* (Ps. 89:16a); and *"Rejoice evermore"* (1 Thess. 5:16).

Rejoice *always, all the day, ever more.* Again, it sounds as though rejoicing is very important. What exactly is rejoicing? The single best overall definition I have found for the word *rejoice* is, "the act of expressing joy." It seems it would be impossible to rejoice without any type *of action* or *expression.* This would be as unnatural as being happy and not smiling. How could we possibly express such strong emotions as thankfulness, love, and joy, without using our physical bodies?

Take a moment to stop reading and try to express any emotion you choose without using your physical body in any way. It's impossible. God created us with emotions, and He gave us bodies with which to express those emotions.

In some of the churches I have visited while in the ministry, it is acceptable to sing, but not too loudly. In others, even clapping while singing was not acceptable. These are traditions that directly oppose the God-given nature of man to worship. The good news is that these churches I just mentioned invited our dance ministry to come as part of their plan to break through these old, binding traditions. I thank God for the many pastors and worship leaders of these traditional churches who are boldly responding to the Spirit and are stepping out to lead their people into deeper levels of worship to God's glory.

Respond to the Father

When I've been away from home, my children are always glad to see me return. They express it by running to me, kissing me, and hugging me. Even if I only went grocery shopping, my two-year-old will squeal with delight to see me return, lovingly saying, "Mama's home, Mama's home! Hawough, Mama, I wuv oo!" He lifts his arms for me to pick him up so he can kiss my face and neck. Even my 16-year-old son comes to me and gives me kisses and hugs during the day, sometimes for no apparent reason at all. I'm glad that no one told my children that it was unacceptable behavior to rejoice in their love for their mother and act out their expression of it.

But the traditions of man have told God's children that it is not acceptable behavior for them to rejoice in their love for their Father and to act in expressing it. Our minds must be renewed on this issue. The body can't respond unless the mind gives it the signal, and our minds have been programmed according to tradition. These traditions do not line up with God's Word, yet they do line up with and support satan's deception. It is far too common for men, women, or children who find it unacceptable to express themselves in church to be welcomed with open arms to freely express themselves at school dances, weddings, bars, and sporting events. Yet to simply lift our hands to a loving God and verbally thank Him is considered totally unacceptable in many churches today.

It only stands to reason, if we are to glorify God in our bodies, then we must move and use them in some fashion. To some, these expressions are thought of as strictly Old Testament, primitive, or even heresy. The apostle Paul writes this in the New Testament concerning his belief system for worship, *"But this I confess unto thee, that after the way which they call heresy, so worship I the God of my fathers, believing all things which are written in the law and in the prophets"* (Acts 24:14). The law and the prophets is the Old Testament, and Paul, a New Testament apostle, endorsed its validity and application to our worship today.

Dancing in the Father's House

Another New Testament example of dancing is found in Jesus' account of the prodigal son. This story is full of beautiful types that are rich in truth. In this story, the father is a type of our heavenly Father.

Therefore, did Jesus make a mistake in saying that there was dancing in the father's house? If the father is a type of God, then the father's house is a type of God's house. In God's house there is dancing.

> *For this my son was dead, and is alive again; he was lost, and is found. And they began to be merry. Now his elder son was in the field; and as he came and drew nigh to the house, he heard music and dancing* (Luke 15:24-25).

This dancing in the father's house was due to the salvation of his child. We must rejoice in the God of our salvation. Salvation is the foundational reason for our dance. Why would I want to praise or worship God in dance if I didn't know His salvation? Why would I want to rejoice in the salvation of another if I didn't understand it myself?

If the members of the father's house in the story of the prodigal son had been bound by the traditions of men today, instead of dancing and making merry at the salvation of the son, they likely would have nodded with a smile as they remained religiously seated. Or at best perhaps, they may have offered quiet verbal congratulations along with a soggy handshake. We must wake up and see that these lethargic reactions do not reflect holiness as we have been previously taught; they only reflect deception and submission to the bondages that the enemy has succeeded in passing off as holy and respectable behavior in the Church.

They Won't Respond

When I first began to search the Scripture concerning God's will for the dance, I started with the most obvious basics. I went to my concordance, looked up the word *dance*, and followed through by reading every Scripture concerning the word. In the New Testament, I came across this Scripture as taught by Jesus:

> *But whereunto shall I liken this generation? It is like unto children sitting in the markets, and calling unto their fellows, and saying, We have piped unto you, and ye have not danced;*

we have mourned unto you, and ye have not lamented (Matthew 11:16-17).

At first I didn't understand what Jesus was getting at, so I asked the Lord, "What does this mean?" I'll never forget His clear and simple response, which He spoke in my spirit. He said, "They won't respond."

The people Jesus referred to in this Scripture would not show any emotions. They would not mourn to express sorrow, and they would not dance to express joy. This is a sad picture of many churches today, for their members hide safely behind masks, never daring to reveal their true feelings. I know what this is like. I remember a time when I sat safely in the back of the church, more of an observer than a participant. From that position, I could see everyone else, and they could not see me. I once heard a man on Christian radio say that church is the only place where people arrive early to get a back seat. I thank God for the fresh moving of His Spirit in these times that the negative truth of this comment is quickly giving way to the sight of eager believers who arrive early to reserve front-row seats.

We must see the danger of choosing to not respond. The enemy has caused us to believe that unresponsiveness is the safest option. But Jesus tells us otherwise. By choosing to not respond or participate, the people in this Scripture passage became observers, and with their observation came opinionated judgmentalism. Jesus continued His description of this generation:

> *For John came neither eating nor drinking, and they say, He hath a devil. The Son of man came eating and drinking, and they say, Behold a man gluttonous, and a winebibber...* (Matthew 11:18-19).

In the eyes of the unresponsive observers of Matthew 11:16-19, it seems that the true men of God could do no right. They judged John the Baptist for not eating, and they judged Jesus for eating. Therefore, Jesus likened this group of people to *those who would not dance* as a symbol of their unresponsiveness. This illustration of judgmentalism is a truth that, sadly, is all too common among those who still choose not to, or perhaps have been taught not to respond to our God in worship.

Danger of Judging

Scripture gives us another example of this in the Old Testament. In the Book of Second Samuel, we see a great processional as the ark of the covenant, a type of the presence of God and His glory, was restored to the house of Israel. King David was full of joy, and he expressed that joy by dancing with all his might before the Lord.

> *And David danced before the Lord with all his might; and David was girded with a linen ephod. So David and all the house of Israel brought up the ark of the Lord with shouting, and with the sound of the trumpet* (2 Samuel 6:14-15).

Next, we see King David's wife, Michal, as a type of one who would not dance. As all the house of Israel rejoiced before the Lord, David's own wife sat back while she observed and judged:

> *And as the ark of the Lord came into the city of David, Michal Saul's daughter* [David's wife], *looked through a window, and saw king David leaping and dancing before the Lord; and she despised him in her heart* (2 Samuel 6:16).

Notice it was through a window that she observed David. The phrase "on the outside looking in" comes to my mind. Michal did not join Israel's celebration of the return of the ark of God's presence. She stayed at home and watched through her window. This is exactly where satan wants to keep God's people—in the position of a deceived observer, believing that is the safest place to be.

When King David returned home, Michal rebuked him, telling him what a fool he had made of himself that day. David's response was clear,

> *…It was before the Lord, which chose me before thy father, and before all his house, to appoint me ruler over the people of the Lord, over Israel:* **therefore will I play before the Lord.**

And I will yet be more vile than thus, and will be base in mine own sight... (2 Samuel 6:21-22).

Dancing before the Lord is a humbling experience; one totally abandons himself to the act of expressing his love and joy to the Lord. It is intimate and personal, and it is not expressed for the sake of the observer. As we have seen, observers are prone to critical judgment. I'm sure King David knew his wife well enough to know that she would not understand or approve of his dancing and that she would think he was foolish. But he did not allow such a thought to hinder his love and its expression to God. I'm thankful that King David didn't shuffle along the street before the ark with his head hung low, wanting to rejoice but quenching the spirit thinking, *I know my wife is watching through the window, and I know she wouldn't approve.* How many of us have put our fear of man before our fear and love of God?

I love David's bold response, as he told his wife in so many words, "If you think this is bad, wait until you see what I am going to do tomorrow."

Michal and those for whom she is a type pay a high price for their choice to observe and judge rather than participate. For Michal, her price in the physical was barrenness:

Therefore Michal the daughter of Saul had no child unto the day of her death (2 Samuel 6:23).

For those who fall into Michal's type of judgmental observation, the price paid is spiritual barrenness. Examples of spiritual barrenness include being incapable of producing offspring or fruit; being empty, lacking, desolate; producing inferior crops; being unproductive in results or gain; dull and unresponsive. May we all take heed from Michal's example.

A few years ago I had a situation take place in my life that somewhat parallels this story of Michal and David. There was a special speaker visiting a church in our city that I really wanted to hear. The night she spoke I was teaching dance classes until 7:30, and the meeting started at 7:00. I was tired from teaching, and I knew I would not get there until at least 8:00. Yet something compelled me to go.

I am good friends with the pastor and worship leader of this church, and I have ministered in dance there many times. I always sit in the front or as close to the front as I can get. As I walked in, the place was packed and I had to take the only seat I could find. This seat was just not me; it was near the back and in the center of a row. When the meeting was over the woman next to me (someone I had never seen before in my life) stood up and said she had to apologize to me. As she hugged me, she began to weep emotionally. Then, as she composed herself, she told me her story.

She said that she had strongly disliked me for quite some time. Every time I visited her church she cringed inside thinking, *Who does this woman think she is coming into our church and dancing like that!* She was very offended by me and felt that my dancing was a display of flesh and nothing but a show I was putting on for the people. At one time she had been so upset that she almost got up and walked out of the meeting.

Next, she told me that over this same period of time her relationship with the Lord had grown weaker and weaker. She had only recently prayed desperately to the Lord to restore her relationship with Him, and He reminded her of the offense she had taken with me and told her that she was wrong in her judgment of my offering of praise to Him.

He also revealed to her that deep in her heart she desired this level of freedom and that she was offended at me for having it. She knew she could go no farther with the Lord without resolving this issue. The Lord told her He was going to bring me back into her life so that she could apologize to me. She told me that when I took the seat right next to her she just shook and her whole body felt like Jell-O inside, for she knew that she had to talk to me. I must say her humility, honesty, and obedience are to be commended.

I spoke to her recently, and she was so free that we laughed and talked about the incident as though it had happened to two other people. Her relationship with the Lord is now flourishing. I pray that this testimony will minister to anyone who is struggling with similar feelings.

God Is Your Defense

One last example to serve both as a warning to those who judge and as an encouragement to those who dance: In Acts 5, Peter and some of the other apostles stood before an angry council who rebuked them for teaching about Jesus after they had been commanded not to. When the apostles' response was, *"We ought to obey God rather than men,"* Scripture tells us that the council was cut to the heart and decided to slay them (see Acts 5:29b,33). There is a spirit that despises those who break tradition in order to move boldly ahead in the Lord, just as Michal *despised* David for his dancing. However, what is precious and personal to me about this passage is that it demonstrates that as we boldly move forward in obedience to God's way, He is our defense. Like a mother bear with her cub, He will rise up and sovereignly defend His people. Just as the council was planning to kill the apostles, God moved in the heart of one of their own members.

> *Then stood there up one in the council, a Pharisee, named Gamaliel, a doctor of the law, had in reputation among all the people, and commanded to put the apostles forth a little space; and said unto them, Ye men of Israel, take heed to yourselves what ye intend to do as touching these men. ...And now I say unto you, Refrain from these men, and let them alone: for if this counsel or this work be of men, it will come to nought: but if it be of God, ye cannot overthrow it; lest haply ye be found even to fight against God* (Acts 5:34-35,38-39).

Dance as God originally intended will be restored to the Church. Its restoration cannot be overthrown by skepticism, judgmentalism, fear, or the traditions of man. Anyone who actively opposes this move of God will be found fighting against God Himself. Those of you who are on the front lines of the restoration of dance, fear not; for *God and His Word are your defense as you praise Him in the dance and glorify Him in your body.* Do not be discouraged by the council of the Pharisees. Press on in obedience to God, for we too ought to obey God rather than man!

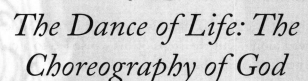

CHAPTER 7

The Dance of Life: The Choreography of God

The Danse
(by Kemper Crabb)

All creation moves in a cosmic danse before the Lord her King; And the rhythms, the reason, the rhyme of the danse pulses within everything.

And the universe wheels and whirls like a dervish in perfect seven-step time. The Lord made the danse, he taught her the steps and he causes the songs to shine.

We must danse, danse, danse, danse in God's honour. We must yield all our steps unto the king. We must danse, danse, danse in God's honour.
Let His praises ring throughout the earth.

Adam and Eve dansed in Eden's environs early in Earth's morning-air. They named all the animals musical names, glorious potentiality shared.

But Lucifer sang out a serpentine song and he offered death's danse as his token. In pausing to listen Adam missed his step:

Earth's harmony in the danse broken. Jesus dansed into the world singing his heavenly song.

He taught the danse to those who would listen and learn as he moved along. But the steps of his danse led to a cross where he died while the haters mocked on.

But he dansed through death's arms and over hell's gate and in three days dansed forth from his tomb.

Thus ring the words to one of my favorite songs as it describes life itself as a dance before our God. On a very large scale, all the planets of the universe spin and twirl in a dance of perfect order and timing according to the design and planned movements of God, the master choreographer of life.

On a much smaller scale, the very makeup and fabric of the human body also moves in a continuous and spontaneous dance of life. The rhythm of our heart beats faithfully day and night without any voluntary assistance on our part, and it pumps life-giving blood to all the living, moving cells of our body. Involuntarily, our lungs expand and contract, breathing the breath of life. We are continually being regenerated as life is constantly created and sustained within us, moment by moment, according to the design and plan of our God.

It is an interesting and eye-opening concept to take a look at the everyday physical movements of our bodies as a dance of life before the Lord. In returning to the song, the words to the chorus graciously sing, "We must danse, danse, danse, danse in God's honour. We must yield all our steps unto the king." This part of the song describes the aspect of the dance of life that I have found to be the most eye-opening of all. We are no longer addressing the spontaneous, involuntary movement of our life's dance, such as our breathing or the beating of our heart. We have now moved into an area that encompasses man's free will, as we consciously choose each movement in our dance of life.

Our dance may be one that honors God throughout the day by yielding our steps in obedience to His Word and the promptings of His Spirit. Perhaps at times our choice of movements may honor self or satan, rather than God, as we seek to fulfill the lust and desires of the flesh in times of selfishness, anger, rebellion, or disobedience. The truth is that the movements of our dance of life are continually in agreement with, and in service to, the honoring of either God, self, or satan.

This is all orchestrated by our free will, for we have been given by God the power to choose and control the movements of our life. What kind of dance will you choose to do? In Psalm 37:23, King David wrote, *"The steps of a good man are ordered by the Lord...."* It is your choice whether or not you will yield your steps to the order and Lordship of the Master Choreographer of life.

The "dance of life" is the test that proves and reveals the true heart of a man, for actions speak louder than words. In choosing Jesus Christ as Lord and yielding our steps to His Lordship, we join the orchestra of eternal life, becoming part of the symphony that glorifies His majesty in the earth.

> *...Bring My sons from far, and My daughters from the ends of the earth; even every one that is called by My name: for I have created him for My glory...* (Isaiah 43:6-7).

In order to fulfill this call to glorify God, it is not enough just to know that you have been accepted as a member of the orchestra. We must become active members and participants under the direction of the orchestra leader, our Creator.

It was interesting and quite surprising to me to learn that the word *orchestra* literally means "to dance." It is also very interesting and quite fitting to this teaching that the word *orchestrate* means "to compose, write down, and arrange for the orchestra" (or dancers). Another definition for *orchestrate* is "to arrange or combine so as to achieve a maximum effect." Can you imagine what the maximum effect would be if we all yielded our steps to the instructions of our orchestra leader, the Master Choreographer of life?

Choreographed Dance

The word *orchestrate* beautifully parallels our English word *choreography*. The word *choreography* consists of the Greek word *choreia*, which means "dance," plus the French word *graphie*, which simply means to "write down." Much like the one who orchestrates, the choreographer writes down, in advance, the directions for the designed, planned steps of a dance, with the purpose of documenting what is good, so it won't be lost or forgotten. He then teaches this information to the dancers with the goal of their dance being presented in unity, order, and beauty that it might achieve the maximum desired effect.

With these definitions, we can beautifully parallel the written Scriptures to the choreography of God for our dance of life. He has written down in advance His directions for the planned steps of a man, with the purpose of documenting what is good, so that it will not be lost or forgotten. His will is that this plan be taught to the dancers of life so their movements may be presented before God in unity, order, and beauty. The psalmist in Psalm 119:133 (AMP) writes, *"Establish my steps and direct them by* [means of] *Your word...."* As Christians, the Word of God is our standard, direction, orchestration, and choreography for life's steps.

As valuable as the Word of God is in directing the steps of our life, it is important to note that the written Word without the ingredient of the Spirit of God can be dangerous: *"...for the letter killeth, but the spirit giveth life"* (2 Cor. 3:6). This is a very important truth in relation to the subject of choreographed dance.

There is a measure of controversy concerning the subject of choreographed dance in the church today. Some people feel that if a dance is not created as a spontaneous, spur-of-the-moment expression, it is not led of the Spirit and should not be included in what is proper or acceptable as dance is being restored in the church. This is a serious accusation and conflict, especially in view of the number of choreographed dances that are being presented in our churches today.

Just because something is conceived and written down in advance does not disqualify it from being spontaneously birthed from the heart of God. If that were true, we would have to throw out the majority of all the sermons ever preached and songs ever written or sung. If you stop and think about it, this kind of thinking would disqualify even the validity of the Word of God. For the Scriptures were written down in advance for our benefit.

It is obvious that not every choreographed dance is of the Spirit of God any more than every sermon that is spoken or song that is sung. Some people are not called to choreograph dance for the Lord, yet they do. Some are not called to preach, to minister in song, or to play musical instruments, yet they do. This attack on the validity of choreographed dance is just that—an attack. The reasoning behind this deception has no solid foundation.

The calling of the choreographer in the house of the Lord is a prophetic gift that should be highly esteemed and valued as God has given these persons the ability to clearly communicate and visually manifest His glory in the demonstration of spirit and power. Anyone who has sat under the anointing of the Spirit-inspired choreographed dance knows that I do not exaggerate in this description. I have personally and continually witnessed, since 1983, the power of the Holy Spirit, as it has been manifested through anointed, choreographed dance, literally set the captives free and bring deliverance to those who are demonically bound.

Once I was invited to minister in a nursing home for the elderly and disabled. I had recently choreographed a dance to Psalm 91, and I felt that this was what I was to share. When we arrived, all the people were gathered in one half of a very large room. In a far corner of the other half of the room sat a very large black man in a wheelchair. Both his legs had been amputated above the knee, and his countenance was wild and disturbing. As one of the attendants noticed me looking over at him, he warned me not to go near the man. He said that the man had very long strong arms and a habit of grabbing hold of people and not letting go.

As soon as the speaker began to teach from the Word, this man became visibly disturbed. He stuck his fingers in his ears, shaking his head violently back and forth. He breathed in and out rapidly through clenched teeth while rocking forward and back in his wheelchair.

When the speaker had finished teaching, I stood up and began to minister Psalm 91 in the language of the dance. I was no longer aware of this man's behavior, for my attention was on the dance. Suddenly, I noticed him wheeling his chair directly into the center of the area designated for the dance. I continued to dance as I carefully directed my steps around his chair. He did not take his eyes off my every move, and he was no longer in a violent frenzy, but rather, he became absorbed in the dance.

When I finished dancing, he began to wheel his chair toward me, yet I felt no fear, only a strong anointing of God's love for him. The man reached out and grabbed hold of me tightly. My arms looked like little white toothpicks in his large black hands.

His countenance had changed from appearing violently disturbed to gentle and loving. I shared how much God loved him and knew all that he had been through in his life from the time he had been born until that moment. He loosened his grip, and with a very concerned look on his face, he began to gently pat my hands. It was hard to understand what he was saying, but as I listened intently, I realized that he had compassionately said, "Your hands are cold."

I stayed and continued to share Jesus with him as he intently stared at me, shaking his head in acknowledgment. Something that had held this man so powerfully captive had been broken through the ministry of God's Word in music and dancing. In this particular case, it was a choreographed dance. Whether this dance had been inspired by God previously for this appointed time or whether it had been created momentarily by the Spirit made no difference in its power.

Whether it's a sermon, a song, a dance, or even the Word of God itself, it has no life without the Spirit of God. The words, notes, or dance movements could be identical, yet without life if they are not ministered in Spirit and in truth. I thank God for the freshness and life-giving power that is spontaneously birthed from the heart of God, whether a dance is momentarily presented or written down in advance for an appointed time.

Choreographed dance is scriptural. There are many specific Jewish dances with choreographed steps that have been handed down and taught and retaught over the ages. In the Old Testament, the temple priest, musicians, singers, and dancers had to submit to five years of apprenticeship training before being allowed to participate as members of the regular chorus.[1] This information suggests that the dancers did more than dance spontaneously every time they met for training over that five-year period.

God is a God of order. In mastering any skill, it is God's desire that we study and polish that talent, developing it to its maximum effect to the glory, honor, and power of God. In fact, this is the responsibility of anyone who is called and appointed to lead God's people in the area of praise and worship.

The most powerful scriptural position of worship leader of which I am aware, other than that of lucifer before his fall, was that of Chenaniah. When King David appointed the singers and musicians to worship before the Ark in First Chronicles 15:16, we see that David spoke to the chief of the Levites (Chenaniah) to appoint brethren to be singers with instruments of music. Scripture clearly states that Chenaniah was chief of the Levites, and that he instructed about the song "...*because he was skilful*" (1 Chron. 15:22).

It would be hard to develop a gift to the point of being addressed as skillful if you never practiced. Becoming skillful is pleasing to God; yet choreographed dance has been criticized for this very characteristic.

I have been training dancers specifically to dance for the glory of God in the house of the Lord since 1987. It is those who have faithfully trained the longest and hardest both physically and spiritually, in answer to the call of God, that have carried the heaviest anointing. Second Timothy 2:15 tells us to *"study to show thyself approved unto God, a workman that needeth not be ashamed, rightly dividing the word of truth."* The ministry of dance presented through choreography as an interpretation and visual picture of God's Word must be handled with respect and honor.

The choreographer of dance in the house of the Lord should be well studied in the written word so that, in turn, he or she may rightly divide the word of truth in and through the expression of dance. Therefore, just as Chenaniah was appointed because he was skillful, so the choreographer must also be skillful.

As valuable as skillfulness may be, there is another ingredient that is just as important. The next parallel between the calling of Chenaniah as a worship leader and the position of the choreographer is found in the definition of the name *Chenaniah*, for it means, "Jah has planted." Yes, Chenaniah was chief of the Levites and was able to become skillful because God had created him for this position. Being skillful alone is not enough when it comes to a specific position in the house of the Lord. You must be *called* to that position. You must be a Chenaniah, one who is *planted of the Lord.*

The choreographer must be in the position of prophetically receiving designed and planned movements from God, the Master Choreographer, so that he or she may communicate His life and His glory through the dance. A truly God-appointed choreographer will not create a dance out of his or her own knowledge or skill, but will prayerfully wait upon the Lord for the inspiration of the Holy Spirit for just the right music and movements.

Let us not quench the flow of this beautiful gift that God is restoring to His glory. Yes, we must discern what is of the Lord and what is counterfeit or even birthed out of ignorance, but we must not throw out the baby with the bathwater. To quote Dr. Fuchsia Pickett in her response to witnessing a choreographed dance presented by my dance troupe, "If God doesn't like the choreographed dance, then why did He show up? He not only showed up; He showed off!"

"Jesus dansed into the world singing his heavenly song. He taught the danse to those who would listen and learn as he moved along." Let's make His praise glorious as we listen, learn, and move along with Him in submission to the orchestra leader and Master Choreographer, yielding all the steps of our everyday life to the Lord of the dance.

Lord of the Dance[2]
(by Sydney Garter)

I danced in the morning when the world was begun, and I danced in the moon and the stars and the sun, and I came down from heaven and I danced on the earth. At Bethlehem I had my birth.

I danced for the scribe and the Pharisee, but they would not dance and they would not follow me; I danced for the fishermen, for James and John; they came to me and the dance went on.

I danced on the Sabbath when I cured the lame, the holy people said it was a shame; they whipped and they stripped and they hung me high; and left me there on a cross to die.

I danced on a Friday and the sky turned black; it's hard to dance with the devil on your back; they buried my body and they thought I'd gone, but I am the dance and I still go on.

They cut me down and I leapt up high, I am the life that'll never, never die; I'll live in you if you'll live in me; I am the Lord of the Dance, said he.

Dance, then, wherever you may be; I am the Lord of the Dance, said he. And I'll lead you all wherever you may be, and I'll lead you all in the dance, said he.

ENDNOTES

1. Samuel L. Sasser, *The Dance—To Be or Not to Be*, 1984.

2. "Lord of the Dance." Words: Sydney Carter. © 1963 Stainer & Bell Ltd. Used by permission of Hope Publishing Co., Carol Stream, IL 60188. All rights reserved. Used by permission.

CHAPTER 8

～

Extreme Worship
and Spiritual Freedom

The word *extreme* when used in context with the word *worship* may automatically trigger a negative reaction by those who might fearfully picture an out-of-control, wildly chaotic worship service. In reality, the word *extreme* is a positive, orderly, biblical description of an intimacy, or depth, of worship that encompasses all that is within us. The word *extreme* is defined as meaning "utmost, in the greatest degree, immoderate, far from what is usual or conventional, very severe, drastic (*superi*)." Worship is the one thing in life that deserves to be done to the utmost, the greatest degree, and for many, a severe and drastic change would be required before our traditional forms of worship could line up with this biblical concept.

The abbreviation *superi*, as previously used in our definition of extreme, is also most appropriate when applied to our worship. *Superi* comes from the word *superlative*, meaning "above, beyond, of the highest kind, quality, or degree." God loves worship of the highest kind, quality, and degree; worship that reaches above and beyond that which is considered moderate. God loves extreme worship. Does this mean that we all have to get up with tambourines, to spin, twirl, and shout? No, not at all. Extreme worship does not necessarily mean dancing with all your might. But it does mean blessing the Lord with all that is within you. King David was indeed a true worshiper who worshiped to the extreme as he cried out, *"Bless the Lord, O my soul: and **all** that is within me..."* (Ps. 103:1).

As we make the sometimes painful transition from tradition to biblical order, our greatest hindrance is that many of us, including myself, come from traditional backgrounds where we were trained from a very young age to sit still and be quiet. This safe and simple formula seemed foolproof for accomplishing the godly order of what appeared to be holy, reverent, and acceptable behavior in our worship services. It is sad but true that many of us, from our earliest days, have spent more time learning *how not* to respond than *how to* respond.

Responding to God is the heart of true worship, and God longs for us to fully and freely respond to Him. Freedom is a vitally important element in true worship. Yet, the very freedom He intimately desires for us has been tragically lost along the way. We must seek to restore freedom in our worship and purpose to fulfill the desire and delight of our Father's heart. The desire of God's heart concerning worship is not inconspicuously hidden in the Scripture somewhere, but is clearly and continuously expressed throughout the Old and New Testaments. The simplest, most basic instructions concerning God's desire for worship tell us that He is seeking those who will worship Him in spirit and truth.

> *But the hour cometh, and now is, when the true worshippers shall worship the Father in spirit and in truth: **for the Father seeketh such to worship Him.** God is a Spirit: and they that worship Him **must** worship Him in spirit and in truth* (John 4:23-24).

Notice this passage says, *"They that worship Him **must** worship Him in spirit and in truth." Must* is a very strong word; therefore, in seeking worship of the highest kind, quality, and degree, it is important for us to begin to understand what God means by spirit and truth. Beginning with the word *spirit*, it is exciting to discover the direct connection between worshiping in spirit and the basic element of *freedom*.

Spirit Equals Freedom

Where the Spirit of the Lord is, there is liberty (2 Corinthians 3:17b).

The word, *liberty*, in the Greek means "freedom." It does not mean we are slaves. The deeper we allow ourselves to respond to the Spirit in our worship, the more freedom we will experience. The liberty that comes in the presence of God is wonderful and exciting, yet at the same time it can be frightening as we step out of our comfort zone and into unfamiliar territory. This is territory that the enemy has worked hard to keep from us. He knows that as we of the Body of Christ humbly yield ourselves to God and venture into this deeper realm, the extreme, superlative worship we speak of will become manifested. Why does the enemy fear this? Because he knows that God can do great and mighty works through totally yielded vessels. The term, *totally yielded*, is of key importance as we seek to worship our God in spiritual freedom.

This is where the response of our physical bodies comes into the picture. We cannot experience total liberty or freedom without using our physical bodies. Man is made up of spirit, soul, and body. In order to yield ourselves totally and completely to God in worship, we must allow the completion of our emotion to be manifested in and through our bodies. We discovered earlier, yet it bears repeating, that without following through in outward expression, an inward emotion will be bound, frustrated, and incomplete. Bondage, frustration, and the dissatisfaction of incompletion do not fulfill the freedom our Father seeks in true worshipers.

Our freedom is a precious, valuable, and costly matter, and it is by no means free. Freedom is something that must be fought for. For mankind, the value of freedom has been directly connected with the high price of death. As Americans, we are all too familiar with the cost of the lives of men and women who have fought and died for the freedom of our nation. Although we are very familiar with this principle, many Americans have yet to understand the one death that has brought freedom for all time to all men in every nation. This freedom is given to us through the sacrificial death of God's own Son on the Cross, and it is more valuable than the natural freedom of our nation. It is a *spiritual freedom* with a price far too high to be paid by any man, or any number of men, at any time. Not only is God a Spirit who must be worshiped in spirit and truth, but man is also a spirit. And there is no true freedom in worship for man without this spiritual freedom that has been purchased for us by Christ.

Reading from the Book of Isaiah, Jesus stood in the synagogue and proclaimed this very issue of freedom. Note that Jesus fully credits His anointing and qualifications to proclaim liberty directly to the *Spirit of the Lord God.*

> *The spirit of the Lord God is upon me, **because the Lord has anointed and qualified me** to preach the Gospel of good tidings to the meek, the poor, and afflicted; He has sent me to bind up and heal the brokenhearted, **to proclaim liberty** to the [physical and spiritual] captives and the opening of the prison and of the eyes to those who are bound* (Isaiah 61:1 AMP).

Just as the Father seeks those who will worship Him in spirit, He seeks those who will worship Him in freedom. There is no true worship without the freedom that comes from the Spirit. Although this freedom of spirit has been given to us through Christ, we have also been given a free will with which we may accept or reject it. Rejecting it is much easier than accepting it; for in accepting it we battle against two basic things: *our flesh and the traditions of men.*

The flesh and Spirit war against one another. The flesh brings bondage and death, while the Spirit brings freedom and life. The traditions of men directly war against the true spiritual freedom God has intended for His people in worship. They bring silence where there should be a shout, distance where there should be intimacy, boredom where there should be excitement, and death where there should be life.

Pressing Through and Reaching Out

This brings to mind the New Testament story about the woman with the issue of blood (see Mark 5:25-34). She knew that if she could only touch Jesus she would be healed. Scripture tells us that a crowd of people followed and "thronged" Jesus. *Thronged* is defined in *Strong's Concordance* as "to compress, i.e., to crowd on all sides." The woman didn't sit down under a tree somewhere and hope that He would come to her. I believe she pressed through the crowd and reached out until she touched the hem of His garment. Jesus didn't walk up to her and place the hem of His garment in her hand. I've always pictured her *pressing through* and *reaching out* to touch it. This is why we lift our hands, kneel, and bow down. It is a pressing through, a reaching out beyond the flesh, beyond the religious traditions of men.

We must put to use this precious gift of freedom and enter into the holy presence of God through the sacrificial blood of the Lamb. Without the revelation of this gift of freedom, we will remain forever bound in our worship.

Additional hindrances to our spiritual freedom are the distracting voices or thoughts that pass through our minds during worship. These distractions remind us of our sin and how unworthy we are to enter into the holy presence of God. However, our answer can always be a resounding, *Not so!* for the blood of Jesus Christ has made us worthy.

> ...*without shedding of blood is no remission.* ...*He appeared to put away sin by the sacrifice of Himself* (Hebrews 9:22b,26).

> ...*we are sanctified through the offering of the body of Jesus Christ once for all.* ...*Having therefore, brethren, boldness to*

enter into the holiest by the blood of Jesus (Hebrews 10:10,19).

This word for *boldness* is defined in the Greek as meaning "liberty." With liberty and freedom we can now enter the holiest place. The word *boldness* in the context of this Scripture is the Greek word *parrhesia*. It is made up of two words: *psa*, meaning "all, every, thoroughly, the whole"; and *rheo*, through the idea of "pouring forth, to utter, speak, or say." Not only has God given us boldness, liberty, and freedom to speak or sing His praise through the expression of our voice, but the very definition of this word suggests our *all, everything, the whole, thoroughly, pouring forth*. This is the picture of the totally yielded vessels for which God longs.

Christ's sacrifice not only purifies and makes acceptable what we think, feel, or speak, but also purifies the presentation of our physical bodies.

*Let us draw near with a true heart in full assurance of faith, having our hearts sprinkled from an evil conscience, and our **bodies** washed with pure water* (Hebrews 10:22).

Let us therefore come boldly unto the throne of grace, that we may obtain mercy, and find grace to help in time of need (Hebrews 4:16).

*For ye are **bought with a price**: therefore glorify God in your body, and in your spirit, which are God's* (1 Corinthians 6:20).

Truth Equals Freedom

*And ye shall know the truth, and the **truth** shall make you free* (John 8:32).

In our quest for worship of the highest kind, quality, and degree, it would be difficult to separate *truth* from the *spirit*, for the Spirit of God is the Spirit of truth. Therefore, worshiping in spirit requires worshiping in truth. This simply means that what we are expressing in our worship through song or movement must be the truth. *"Let us draw near with a true heart..."* (Heb. 10:22).

If I suddenly dropped to my knees and covered my face during worship simply because I saw someone else do it and thought it looked spiritual, then that expression would not be the truth. Movement in worship is not for the sake of movement. It must be a true, honest expression of the heart. The perfect, honest, and complete expression of a particular moment may result in something as simple as one gentle tear. If that tear is the perfect expression of that particular emotion at that moment, done in spirit and truth, then God is glorified in the highest quality and degree of worship.

Sometimes in the presence of God, we are so overwhelmed by His glory that we cannot speak or move. Sometimes we cannot even stand in His presence and we fall to our knees or lie prostrate on the floor. This is giving God extreme glory. God desires honest, truthful expression from honest, truthful emotions. This kind of expression, whether it be a single tear, a lifted hand, a graceful dance, or even a wildly enthusiastic dance that is performed with all one's might, if it is done in spirit and truth, it brings extreme, superlative glory of the highest quality and degree. It encompasses and expresses all that is within and accomplishes complete fulfillment.

Worshiping in truth eliminates all religious ritualistic expression that is acted out simply because someone taught it to you as the expected thing to do at a dictated time. Genuflecting, making the sign of the Cross, even lifting your hands, although genuine expressions, are frequently nothing more than ritual. God alone knows our hearts, but when we have been taught to express meaningful movement on command as part of a religious program, we become robbed of the beauty and holiness that these movements were originally intended to express when they are birthed out of true humility, love, adoration, and reverence to God. If your worship is simply acted out by obligation or religious tradition, it becomes null and void and does not qualify as worshiping in spirit and truth. It is the truth that sets us free, and we must know the truth and walk in it in order to experience the freedom provided for us in worship.

Complete Abandon

Back in the spring of 1984, the Lord taught me something about freedom in worship through a simple object lesson. My bedroom is on the second floor of a tall, two-story house, and the window next to my bed places my view at the same level as the treetops. Our room faces a large woods with many different species of birds.

Quite often that spring, for some reason, birds from far and wide came and congregated in our woods. It seemed as though each picked a limb at the edge of our woods, and they were perched together facing my bedroom window like a giant choir. As the clock tolled 5:30 A.M., they let loose. Because they always chose this early hour to conduct their session, I found myself quickly closing the window, attempting to muffle this very loud concert and gain a little more sleep.

I'll never forget one particular morning because just as I was about to get up, the Lord told me to listen and learn. As I lay there, it was as though I was listening to a heavenly praise choir that was perfectly orchestrated and directed. These birds were praising the Lord with all that was within them, and no two birds were exactly the same. It reminded me somewhat of when we sing in the Spirit. I say only somewhat, because as I listened, there was one vital thing the Lord impressed upon me to learn from these birds.

It was a pure and glorious praise *of complete abandon*, as they individually sang their little hearts out. Not one bird worried about what the other birds were thinking, wearing, or doing. They obviously did not care what time it was, and not one was suppressed, depressed, or oppressed. The birds were not concerned with race, color, or denomination. There was just a beautiful, heavenly unity.

The Lord spoke to me and said, "This is how I want you to praise Me in the dance, and this is how I want you to sing." The Lord desires a complete abandon of self, a complete sacrifice of all that is within us in order to magnify and glorify Him—spirit, soul, and body. This is extreme worship of the highest kind, quality, and degree. It is immoderate, for it reaches above and beyond what is considered usual or conventional. I urge you as well; the next time you hear a bird singing its little heart out, stop, listen, and learn.

CHAPTER 9

～

Dance and the Anointing

Any attempt to execute the dance as a ministry without the anointing is nothing more than skillful movement to Christian music. We must reiterate that the dance in itself is amoral—neither good nor evil. It is not dance itself that has the power to break spiritual bondages but the anointing of God as it works through the dance as a vehicle and administrator of that anointing.

The role of dance in ministry is much like that of a telephone wire. The wire in itself is dead, having no power of its own to produce the necessary electricity for communicating valuable messages from one point to another, yet it was perfectly designed to transport these messages by means of the electricity running through it. I have witnessed so-called dance ministry that amounted to nothing more than a disconnected phone line; it attempted to deliver a message that was never received. This is the effect of dance without God's anointing. I have also gloriously participated in, as well as witnessed, dance that clearly connected man and God. This type of dance delivered and administered the anointing through a powerfully charged connection.

A Piece of the Whole

It is critically important that we take time to seek understanding concerning the anointing and its vital necessity in the true restoration of dance. Although God's ways are simple, gaining understanding of them can sometimes seem complex. To remedy this, Jesus often used common object lessons called parables to teach these truths. Concerning the anointing and its connection with the dance, God has given me the illustration of a common children's puzzle to help bring understanding in this area.

One day my daughter, Abigail, asked if I would help her put together one of her puzzles. I agreed, and because it was such a beautiful day, we decided to take it out on the deck. Working side by side, we enjoyed watching the brightly colored picture come together. We were almost finished when we realized that we couldn't find the last piece. We looked and looked and finally decided that it must have been missing before we started. We were both very disappointed that we would not be able to complete the picture. In fact, if we had known a piece was missing, we would not have chosen to do that puzzle in the first place.

There is something disturbing about a puzzle with missing pieces. I believe it has something to do with our sense of order, for God is obviously a God of order and we were created in His image. There is something about order that brings a feeling of satisfaction and completeness. The missing puzzle piece left us feeling dissatisfied, incomplete, and disappointed. It was just a puzzle, and our disappointment was only momentary, but I began to feel impressed that there was a lesson in all this.

We ended up throwing that puzzle away. It seemed a shame, but we did not want to take the time to put it together again only to see an incomplete picture. A few days later, I found the missing piece on the ground underneath the deck. It was still like new, all brightly colored, as it lay there alone in the dirt. I couldn't quite figure out what part of the puzzle it completed, for by itself it didn't seem to make much sense, and without the rest of the puzzle it was worthless.

That day, God began to unfold some beautiful truths to me concerning dance and its proper place in the Body of Christ. Just like a puzzle, God has a master plan, and every piece is important to the overall picture. Dance is one of those important puzzle pieces, and for far too long it has not been recognized as belonging to the picture at all. God is not pleased at a puzzle with a missing piece any more than we are. Without the gift of dance, God's overall picture is incomplete.

Not only does dance belong as a functioning, valuable part of God's picture, but, equally as important, it needs to be properly connected and fitly joined with the other parts of the picture as God originally designed and intended it to be. Understanding and perfecting this relationship is definitely not an overnight process. Unfortunately, we can often miss the mark. But much of this can be avoided with proper teaching from the Word of God.

In our studies, we must be careful not to narrow our focus and study dance as one, isolated puzzle piece. This can far too easily lead to worshiping the creation rather than the Creator. We need a balanced message with our focus upon the proper function of dance as a part of the overall plan of God. So far we have only received a tiny glimpse of His plan, and we have not begun to understand the full function of dance in the Church. We must realize that this gift will only function properly when it is properly connected in the Body of Christ. This principle of being *properly connected* is a vital foundational truth. Without an understanding and proper application of this principle, the dance will never enter the fullness of God's original intention for it.

God used my experience with Abby's puzzle to bring understanding that each puzzle piece or ministry gift, such as dance, is a part of God's overall plan. Unless each piece is properly connected, it will not function to its fullness. This fullness is the anointing of God in our ministry, which, when properly connected, flows freely, coming directly from Christ who is the head through us, the members of His Body.

In God's Word, the human body is used as a type to help us understand our oneness in Christ. The head is Christ, and every body part is a type of each individual's function in the Church as we work together to make up the entire Body of Christ. Christ no longer walks the earth in a single, human body as He did for that short 33-year period. As we submit to Christ as Lord, we ourselves become Christ's Body here and now. We thereby begin to function together to further the workings of the Kingdom of God.

In continuing this lesson, I have listed four things that can happen to affect the functioning of the gift of dance in relation to the Body of Christ. It can be:

~ Disconnected.
~ Dislocated—Stage I.
~ Dislocated—Stage II.
~ Divinely (properly) connected.

Disconnected

Remember that lost puzzle piece I found under the deck? This piece is a type of worldly dance. It was separated and completely disconnected from its proper original place in the puzzle, just as worldly dance is disconnected from and has nothing whatsoever to do with the Body of Christ. The piece was very brightly colored and appealing, just as worldly dance can appeal to our senses. But, remember, without the rest of the puzzle, that solitary piece had no purpose or true value.

Although the role of the worldly dancer has obviously no effect or function in the furthering of the ministry of the Body of Christ, this is not to say that worldly dance has no effect at all. It can be powerfully effective in furthering, supporting, and promoting the attributes of the kingdom of this world such as lust, sex, sin, sensuality, demon worship, or even just self-ability and skill.

We were all created and originally designed to be functioning members of the Body of Christ. Those who do not know Christ, or choose to reject Christ, are disconnected. Without proper connection and relationship, they are walking in a state of perversion. You may think that the word *perversion* is a little strong until you see the truth in light of the standard of God's Word. If we were created and originally designed to be functioning members of Christ's Body but are not connected and functioning within that Body, then we have either misinterpreted the truth or been led astray by lies. Either way, we are turned away from God's original purpose. The word *pervert* is defined as "to turn from its proper purpose, to misinterpret, to lead astray, to corrupt." It describes one who has deviated from the normal, especially from right to wrong. The word *pervert* comes from the Latin *per*, meaning "thoroughly," and *verterie*, meaning "to turn."

Those who have chosen to become members of the Body of Christ have chosen life, but those who have chosen to reject Christ as the word *pervert* defines have, again, thoroughly turned from God's original purpose of life, which is not only life more abundant but life eternal. As we choose Christ, we not only receive life unto ourselves, but we, in turn, minister life unto others in the Kingdom of God. The disconnected, worldly dancer does not and cannot minister life.

Try to imagine what would happen if your arm was completely disconnected at the shoulder. Disconnected from its life source, that body part would die. It could no longer receive life; therefore, it would become dead and useless to any function concerning that body. This is a clear picture and type of the worldly dancer. Simply stated, that dancer cannot give something he or she does not have to give. Therefore, a dancer who is disconnected from Christ's Body cannot minister or give the life that comes from Christ.

He that hath the Son hath life; and he that hath not the Son of God hath not life (1 John 5:12).

Ephesians 4:18-25 beautifully expresses the devastating condition of being disconnected from the life of God:

Their moral understanding is darkened and their reasoning is beclouded. [They are] alienated (estranged, self-banished) from the life of God [with no share in it; this is] because of the ignorance (the want of knowledge and perception, the willful blindness) that is deep-seated in them, due to their hardness of heart [to the insensitiveness of their moral nature]. In their spiritual apathy they have become callous and past feeling and reckless, and have abandoned themselves [a prey] to unbridled sensuality, eager and greedy to indulge in every form of impurity [that their depraved desires may suggest and demand]. But you did not so learn Christ! Assuming that you have really heard Him and been taught by Him, as [all] Truth is in Jesus [embodied and personified in Him], strip yourselves of your former nature [put off and discard your old unrenewedself] which characterized your previous manner of life and becomes corrupt through lusts and desires that spring from delusion; and be constantly renewed in the spirit of your mind [having afresh mental and spiritual attitude], and put on the new nature (the regenerate self) created in God's image, [Godlike] in true righteousness and holiness. Therefore, rejecting all falsity and being done now with it, let every one express the truth with his neighbor, for we are all parts of one body and members one of another (Ephesians 4:18-25 AMP).

Lack of knowledge or perception and even willful blindness due to the hardness of one's heart can lead to unbridled sensuality and impurity. These are all parallels and types of worldly dance.

If you are reading this and you are currently in a state of disconnection—you do not know Christ, or perhaps you know of Him but are not serving Him—remember, it has been God's plan from the very beginning for you to use the abilities with which He has gifted you to serve Him. The decision to do so is yours.

For he that soweth to his flesh shall of the flesh reap corruption; but he that soweth to the Spirit shall of the Spirit reap life everlasting (Galatians 6:8).

The dance has been disconnected from its original purpose long enough. It is now beginning to be recognized as a God-given gift, and it has begun to function within the Body of Christ. As with any and every gift, it must not only be connected, but it also must be properly connected in order to fulfill its function and purpose, which leads us to our next point.

Dislocated – Stage I

Being dislocated is definitely a step up from being disconnected, for now you are a connected, living member of the Body of Christ. Even so, this state does not fulfill the purpose of God's overall plan. For it is possible to have living, connected body parts and still be dysfunctional due to an improper or faulty connection.

Webster's dictionary defines *dislocated* as "to put out of place or out of joint; to upset the normal working of." Whenever a body part is dislocated, it not only disrupts the normal working of that part, but it also causes pain to the rest of body as well. Christ, as head of the Body, knows what we were designed for and what we were created to function in. If we would all submit to His order and get in our proper places, the Body would function powerfully in completing the plan of God. Christians often struggle to function in ministries to which they were not called. This too is a type of dislocation.

Have you ever picked up a piece of a puzzle that you were working on only to find yourself trying to force the piece into a space where it didn't belong? When my oldest son was two years old, he had a simple wooden puzzle that consisted of four pieces: an apple, banana, pear, and a cluster of grapes. Whenever he got one of the pieces in the right place, I would clap and praise him, cheering, "Yeah, yeah!" One day he was trying to fit the apple into the pear space, but, of course, there was no way it was going to fit. He pressed and pounded. In frustration he began to cry, saying, "I want 'yeah!' I want 'yeah!'"

This is so much like our desire to please God; we want "yeah!" Yet often we try to force who we are and what we were created to do into the wrong space. Even if you could—and some do—force your puzzle piece into the wrong location, its connections and pattern would be all wrong, for God has created us and ordained each of us for specific works.

> *For we are His workmanship, created in Christ Jesus unto good works, which God hath **before ordained** that we should walk in them* (Ephesians 2:10).

The word *ordained* means "to decree, to destine, to appoint, to admit to the Christian ministry, to confer holy orders upon." Do you want to waste your time forcing your puzzle piece into someone else's space? The entire time you would be dysfunctional, and your ministry would be lifeless, causing disorder in your life as well as in those of the other Body members. This dislocation upsets the normal working of the Body. As Christians, we are commissioned to bring all to salvation in Christ, yet as dislocated dysfunctional members, we may be doing just the opposite.

Let's say, for example, that God has ordained, or as the definition says, "conferred holy orders upon," you to be in children's ministry. Through obedience to this call, you would become properly connected. The life of Christ would freely flow through you to the children in exactly the way each individual child needed. You would be a gatherer unto Christ, leading those children to eternal life. Christ would be shaping and molding their future lives and decisions through you. The very child who might have otherwise turned out to be a drug addict, thief, or even a murderer, may make completely different decisions because of your obedience in your calling.

But let's say that even though you know you are very gifted with children, you decide that you'd much rather be a part of the dance ministry instead. After all, you had a few years of tap and ballet lessons when you were younger, and you are always one of the first to jump to your feet and dance during praise and worship. Now, because the dance ministry is relatively new to the Church, often the understanding of the seriousness of dance as a ministry with a calling is not clearly understood. As a result, all those who are willing are welcome to join the dance team and praise the Lord through that means.

However, this is a misunderstanding between the right and privilege we all have to dance—if we so feel led in congregational worship—and the actual calling of a ministry in the dance. There is a definite difference between the two.

For example, I love to praise the Lord with my singing, and I would never want to be told that I was not allowed to worship God in this way; but by the same token, I would definitely be out of order if I were to run up on the platform during worship, grab a microphone, and begin to lead the congregation in song. First of all, I am not called to do that. Second, this would be completely interrupting to the ministry of the one who is called to it. We understand and respect the ministry of those who are called to lead worship in music and singing. Now we need to be brought to an understanding and respect for those who are called to lead worship in the ministry of the dance.

Time after time, people have approached me after I have danced with a deep desire to express to me how God had ministered through the dance. Many times this was because they were completely surprised; they had never expected God to move through something like dance. Perhaps dance was something they had only ever associated with sin, but with *one short dance*, God completely convinced them otherwise. This is a wonderful tribute to the anointing of God that can flow through the dance. On the other hand, we must also consider the damage that can be done by having dancers who are not called to dance in front of the church. This kind of presentation can cause those who questioned this ministry in the first place to now become convinced—in *one short dance*—that the church is no place for dance.

Just like a puzzle piece in the wrong place cannot contribute to the full picture, so a dislocated member of the Body cannot function in the full anointing of God when that person has been called to operate in a different gift or ministry. This is not the only form of dislocation, however. There is also another type that must still be addressed—Stage II of dislocation.

Dislocated – Stage II

Returning to our puzzle analogy, there are often times when we know that we have found the right piece and we know that we have found the right location in which it fits, but it may take us several tries of turning and adjusting before that piece will slip into place with all its sides properly connected. There is only one way in which the piece will properly fit. Even though we have finally found the right slot, the piece will not be properly connected if we try to put it in upside down, sideways, or backward—no matter how hard we try. Again, the piece will only fulfill its designed function by fitting in one way, according to the master design. For each of us, there is only one master design, only one way—Christ's way. Only when we are properly and fully connected to the Body is the connection with the Head fully clear. Only then can the anointing freely flow from the Head down through the Body.

Let's say you are sure that God has created you to minister in the dance. He has given you assurance and confirmation of that in your heart. You have decided to be obedient and begin to operate in this ministry. Please understand that even then you can still be functioning in a state of dislocation. If my arm is dislocated, that does not mean it is connected to my leg somewhere. *Dislocation* most commonly means out of joint, or not properly connected. Being gifted and called are two very important factors, but you must also allow God to prepare you.

Dance is a ministry that goes far beyond having the ability to dance. It is a calling that requires you to love God with all your heart, soul, mind, and strength. It also requires sensitivity and total submission to the leading of the Spirit. These things come only through a mature relationship with God, which is the primary, basic necessity for your ministry. I strongly caution those who want to quickly launch out: Do not attempt to operate in the fullness of dance ministry without first taking time to develop that relationship. This is something I refer to as *zeal without knowledge* (see Rom. 10:2).

Yes, you may have a love for God. In fact, it may be a very zealous love, yet if you have not taken time in God's Word, growing up in the knowledge of God, you may very well cause the same type of damage to the ministry of dance that we saw caused by one who was not called at all. I know I used this Scripture earlier in the book, but it is one that bears repeating. *"Desire without knowledge is not good, and to be over-hasty is to sin and miss the mark"* (Prov. 19:2 AMP).

> *For I bear them record that they have a zeal of God, but not according to knowledge. For they being ignorant of God's righteousness, and going about to establish their own righteousness, have not submitted themselves unto the righteousness of God* (Romans 10:2-3).

Because the restoration of dance as a ministry in the church is relatively new, there have been many cases of zeal without knowledge. There seems to be a great lack of understanding concerning the ministry of dance as a holy, God-appointed ministry. Being a good musician does not make you a worship leader. Being a good speaker does not make you a pastor, and being a good dancer does not make you a dance minister—even if you are a Christian. God's ways are not our ways. God is not concerned with exterior appearances; it is an interior work that is the foundation for the proper functioning of a ministry. Therefore, the first step in becoming properly connected is to submit yourself humbly to God. Take time to become built up spiritually in the knowledge and love of God before jumping in with both feet, only to find out that you do not know how to swim or even tread water in this area. Too many Christians have witnessed this zealous launching out and sudden drowning in what was intended to be an anointed ministry in dance.

With the understanding that neither being disconnected or dislocated will fulfill the purpose of God, let's move on to the final state of function in this gift, that of one who is divinely, or properly, connected.

Divinely Connected

One night, as I was watching a television program called "Rescue 911," the story was told of a young girl who fell through a window and almost completely cut off her arm. The doctor commented on the complexity of reconnecting her arm. He said that in a case like this one, he could not just sew the arm back together, but there were muscles, arteries, veins, tendons, and nerves that all had to be properly connected in order for the girl to regain full use of her arm.

Just as all these intricate aspects of the inner body needed to be lined up and properly connected for that young girl's arm to be effectively restored, so the many spiritual areas of our lives must be lined up and divinely connected according to the guidance and direction of God's holy Word before effective, anointed ministry can take place.

> *All scripture is given by inspiration of God, and is profitable for doctrine, for reproof, for correction, for instruction in righteousness: that the man of God may be perfect, thoroughly furnished unto all good works* (2 Timothy 3:16-17).

God's Word is our standard, bringing unity between the Head and the Body. I could not easily address the unity of the Body through proper connection with the Head without teaching on the anointing, for they are the same. Let me explain. We've all heard terms used like *the anointing* or *being anointed*. However, I remember the first time that someone came up to me and told me I was an anointed dancer; I didn't know what it meant. In fact, several years passed before God began to reveal to me what anointing really means.

I believe that when we finally discover our calling and finally fit our puzzle piece properly into the puzzle His way, then His anointing will flow in our ministry. Remember how the lost, disconnected puzzle piece made no sense by itself and was of no true value? Well, once that piece is properly slipped into place, it not only comes alive itself, but it helps to bring the surrounding pieces to life—producing one clear picture. This illustrates the unity of the Body communicating the clear message of Christ. This clear message is the anointing.

Strong's Concordance defines *Christ* as, "the anointed one." *Anointed* in the Greek is defined as, 1. "through the idea of contact; 2. to consecrate to an office or religious service." 3. to smear or rub with oil.

Let's take a moment to briefly clarify this definition:

1. "Through the idea of contact"—we in ourselves have no anointing. It is only as we are in clear contact with Christ that the anointing will flow.

2. "To consecrate to an office or a religious service"— In order to function in the anointing, you must be operating in your God-ordained, consecrated office of religious service. Do not attempt to step outside of your calling; it will not be anointed.

3. "To smear or rub with oil"—Oil is the scriptural, physical type of the anointing.

The Oil of Anointing

Behold, how good and how pleasant it is for brothers to dwell together in unity! It is like the precious oil upon the head, coming down upon the beard, even Aaron's beard, coming down upon the edge of his robes (Psalm 133:1-2 NASB).

The first verse of this passage declares that it is good and pleasant for us to dwell together in unity, and we know that there is no unity in a body that has disconnected, dislocated members. However, the second verse tells us what it is like when we all begin to function in our proper places. The word *like* here means "the same as." This psalm says that unity is the same as *"the precious oil upon the head."* What is this precious oil a type of?

> *And you shall make of these a holy anointing oil, a perfume mixture, the work of a perfumer; it shall be a holy anointing oil. ...And you shall anoint Aaron and his sons, and consecrate them, that they may minister as priests to Me* (Exodus 30:25,30 NASB).

The precious oil is a type of the anointing. As Aaron and his sons were consecrated to be priests and ministers unto the Lord, they became mediators through whom the message of God was delivered to the people. As ministers in the Body of Christ, we are called to be priests and mediators. We must be in proper connection with the Head so that we may, in turn, administer the anointing to flow from the Head as an oil to the Body. The oil is the anointing of Christ.

The anointing oil ran from the head (Christ) and flowed first down to the beard. The beard is a spiritual type indicating maturity. Next, we see it flowed down to the edge of Aaron's robes. The word *edge* is the same Hebrew word used for *mouth*, and the word for *robes* here is Hebrew for the word *extension*. This shows us that the biblical order of the flow of the anointing begins with the Head, which is Christ. It next flows through the mature elders, the high priests who are an extension of His mouth, to the Body of Christ.

> *Upon man's flesh shall it not be poured, neither shall ye make any other like it, after the composition of it: it is holy, and it shall be holy unto you* (Exodus 30:32).

Notice these verses do not mention the anointing oil at any time coming in contact with the flesh. In fact, Exodus 30:32 says, *"Upon man's flesh shall it not be poured."* Whether we are disconnected *from* the Body or dislocated *in* the Body, there is no anointing, for these are both types of operating in the flesh. Scripture also says, "*...neither shall ye make any other like it, after the composition of it: it is holy, and it shall be holy unto you*" (Exod. 30:32). This speaks of copying or counterfeiting the true anointing. A dance dress, ballet shoes, and a tambourine with ribbons is not the formula for an anointed dancer. Dance is a serious ministry; its anointing is holy unto the Lord. It is not to be carelessly copied or counterfeited.

In this ministry, Christ's anointed touch can flow like oil from His head down and through the unified members of His Body only through a properly connected Body member. Only a properly connected member has the necessary, clear contact with Christ that must be established to flow in this unity. Unity is the key word. When we humbly submit to the Lord Jesus Christ as the Head of His Body, lining ourselves up with our calling in accordance with His Word, then we will see the manifestation of Christ in the fullness of His anointing. There should be no desire for dance without the anointing in our churches.

CHAPTER 10

~

Spiritual Warfare and the Dance

If the enemy could remove just one chapter from this book, I believe this would be the one. For this chapter exposes a dimension of truth concerning the dance that adversely affects him. Although the dance has been created with many wonderful attributes, I must say it has been particularly exciting for me to discover the power and effectiveness of the dance in spiritual warfare. When unfolding this revelation scripturally, it is important that we first establish that praise and worship are powerful weapons of spiritual war. After this, we will proceed to discover the important role dance plays as a vital element and how it contributes to a victorious outcome in the spiritual warfare aspect of our praise and worship.

Although praise and worship are powerful weapons of war, applying them does not create a foolproof formula. One cannot simply say, "Praise the Lord," and have all his or her troubles disappear. There was always great prayer, faith, and humility, along with the true heartfelt praise and worship, that caused the praises of God's people to be powerful weapons against their enemies. These principles of truth are outlined in Second Chronicles 20, where we find King Jehoshaphat facing the approach of a great army of enemies.

1. Prayer

   *Then Jehoshaphat feared, and set himself [determinedly, as his vital need] to seek the Lord; he proclaimed a fast in all Judah. And Judah gathered to ask help from the Lord; even out of all the cities of Judah they came to **seek the Lord, [yearning for Him with all their desire]** (2 Chronicles 20:3-4 AMP).*

2. Faith

   *If evil comes upon us, the sword of judgment, or pestilence, or famine, we will stand before this house and before You—-for Your Name [and the symbol of Your presence] is in this house—and cry to You in our affliction, **and You will hear and save** (2 Chronicles 20:9 AMP).*

3. Humility

   *O our God, will You not exercise judgment upon them? For we have no might to stand against this great company that is coming against us. **We do not know what to do, but our eyes are upon You** (2 Chronicles 20:12 AMP).*

   The Spirit of the Lord came upon Jahaziel with a word for the people: They were not to fear; for the battle was not theirs but God's, and He would deliver them.

4. Worship and Praise

   *And Jehoshaphat bowed his head with his face to the ground, and all Judah and the inhabitants of Jerusalem **fell down before the Lord, worshiping Him.** And some Levites of the Kohathites and the Korahites stood up to praise the Lord, the God of Israel, with a very loud voice (2 Chronicles 20:18-19 AMP).*

This preparation of the people gave them the faith to do something that, in the natural, seemed nothing short of foolish. King Jehoshaphat appointed, not his mightiest warriors, but instead, singers and praisers to go out before the army saying, "…*Give thanks to the Lord, for His mercy and loving-kindness endure forever!"* (2 Chron. 20:21 AMP) Facing this great and mighty army against whom they previously claimed they had no strength to stand, they now *advanced* with nothing more than faith in their hearts and the praises of God on their lips.

Jehoshaphat had received God's strategic plan for victory over the enemy. Was it to pull out the biggest swords and put on the thickest armor? Yes it was, but not in the natural: *"For the weapons of our warfare are not carnal, but mighty through God to the pulling down of strong holds"* (2 Cor. 10:4).

> *And when they began to sing and to praise, the Lord set ambushes against the men of Ammon, Moab, and Mount Seir who had come against Judah, and they were [self-] slaughtered* (2 Chronicles 20:22 AMP).

Not only did this faithful demonstration of praise *protect* the people from the enemy, but it also *destroyed the enemy.* This is a true principle, a hidden treasure, and something satan desperately wants to prevent us from understanding.

Praise Brings Freedom

Remember Paul and Silas? In the Acts chapter 16, they were seized and taken before the magistrates for preaching, teaching, and demonstrating the gospel. Their clothing was ripped off, they were severely beaten, they were thrown into prison, and their feet were placed in shackles. In the face of what may have appeared to be defeat, Paul and Silas, like Jehoshaphat's army, prayed and praised.

> *But about midnight, as Paul and Silas were praying and singing hymns of praise to God, and the [other] prisoners were listening to them, suddenly there was a great earthquake, so that the very foundations of the prison were shaken; and at once all the doors were opened and everyone's shackles were unfastened* (Acts 16:25-26 AMP).

Paul and Silas did not sit in the prison complaining about the pain of their whip marks or whining that their shackles were too tight. They didn't become discouraged and say, "Christianity is just not worth it." Instead, they began to pray and praise God, whom they loved and trusted in every situation.

As they praised, the very foundation of the prison was suddenly shaken. The prison doors were flung open, and the shackles fell from their feet. Praise God, these biblical principles are as powerfully effective today as they were for Paul and Silas. I thank God that as the Church is discovering new levels of freedom in worship, the foundations of satan (his strongholds) are being shaken and destroyed.

We also must not overlook the power that praise has to free not only those who are praising, but also those who are listening. Acts 16:25 (AMP) points out that *"the* [other] *prisoners were listening to them."* And the following verse states that *"everyone's shackles were unfastened."* This principle becomes powerfully effective as the atmosphere of praise and worship is manifested. Such worship is spiritual warfare against those things that hold us captive, not only for the worshiper, but for the witnesses as well.

King Saul benefited from this principle of being a listener in the presence of praise when he was troubled by an evil spirit:

> *And it came to pass, when the evil spirit from God was upon Saul, that David took an harp, and played with his hand: so Saul was refreshed, and was well, and the evil spirit **departed from him*** (1 Samuel 16:23).

The evil spirit departed from Saul because of the music David played. Saul was left refreshed and well. Scripture tells us that God inhabits the praises of His people (see Ps. 22:3). Ushering in the presence of God through our praise and worship is like turning on a light in a dark room: There is no competition, for where there is light, there is no darkness. Scripture tells us, *"Submit yourselves therefore to God. Resist the devil, and he will flee from you"* (James

4:7). *Submit* to and *resist* are key words here. When we submit to God's direction in the Word concerning the principles of praise and worship, we are also resisting the devil and his spiritual onslaught against us by using weapons that God specifically designed for our victory and satan's defeat.

The examples we have just examined are not fairy tales; they are true historic happenings that are documented in the Word of God. Some people try to dismiss the fact that these same principles hold as true for us today as they did for King Jehoshaphat, Paul, Silas, and King Saul. We must stand strong in our faith, knowing that God is the same yesterday, today, and forever (see Heb. 13:8), and so is the power of praise as a destructive force against the enemy.

Spiritual Warfare and Dance—The Basic Foundation

Now that we have laid a basic scriptural foundation concerning the connection between spiritual warfare and our praise and worship, we can begin to add some additional ingredients, progressively revealing a direct connection between spiritual warfare and the dance.

Some of the most clear and concise information concerning the dance and its function for the Church in this area is found in Psalms 149 and 150. As we begin with the milk and advance to the meat of this matter, we have four foundational building blocks consisting of the following: 1. *who* is to praise; 2. *where* to praise; 3. *how* to praise; and, 4. *why* to praise.

1. *Who*

Building block number one is short and simple—who is to praise God? Psalm 149:2 states, *"Let Israel rejoice in Him that made him: let the children of Zion be joyful in their King."* If you think this doesn't apply to you because it speaks of Israel and Zion, you must understand that Christ broke through the separation of Jew and Gentile—we are one in Christ. As believers, we are all God's people.

*There is [now no distinction] neither Jew nor Greek, there is neither slave nor free, there is not male and female; **for you are all one in Christ Jesus**. And if you belong to Christ [are in Him Who is Abraham's Seed], then you are Abraham's offspring and [spiritual] heirs according to the promise* (Galatians 3:28-29 AMP).

*But he is a Jew who is one **inwardly**, and [true] circumcision is **of the heart**, a spiritual and not a literal [matter]...* (Romans 2:29 AMP).

These following Old Testament verses apply spiritually to us today. Psalm 149:5 says, *"Let the saints be joyful in glory...."* Again, we are the saints. Psalm 149:3 states, *"Let them praise His name in the dance...."* "Them" in this verse refers to the people of God, the saints, Zion, Israel—which we have just seen consists of all those whose hearts have been circumcised and who are heirs according to the promise. If you are a believer, this includes you. If you still question the application of these verses in connection with yourself, there is one last verse that shows this definitely includes everyone: Psalms 150:6 says, *"Let **every thing that hath breath** praise the Lord. Praise ye the Lord."*

Who is to praise Him? You are!

2. *Where*

Building block number two is equally short and simple. It is *where* we are to praise Him, or in this case, where it is scriptural to praise the Lord in the dance. I have never yet heard an argument against dancing before the Lord in the privacy of your home. It is the issue of dance in the church sanctuary that has been so controversial, but we must realize that it is unscriptural to prohibit the dance from the church setting. Psalm 149:1 tells us that we are to praise the Lord in the *"congregation of saints."* The congregation of the saints is anywhere that the saints congregate, which generally is the church sanctuary. We also have a double confirmation as we move to verse 1 of Psalm 150, which states, *"...Praise God in His **sanctuary**...,"* and continues in verse 4, saying, *"Praise Him* *with the timbrel and dance....*" The sanctuary is the church setting. Where are we to praise Him? God's clear desire is for dance to be presented in His sanctuary, among the congregation of saints.

3. *How*

Building block number three, *how* to praise Him, breaks down into what I call the basic four cornerstones of worship, which are the following:

~ The Word of God.

~ Singing.

~ Musical Instruments.

~ Dance.

The Word of God

"Let the high praises of God be in their mouth, and a twoedged sword in their hand" (Psalm 149:6). The two-edged sword is the Word of God (see Heb. 4:12; Rev. 1:16).

Singing

Praise ye the Lord. Sing unto the Lord a new song.... ...Let them sing praises unto Him.... ...Let them sing aloud upon their beds (Psalm 149:1,3b,5b).

Musical Instruments

Let them sing praises unto Him with the timbrel and harp (Psalm 149:3b).

Praise Him with the sound of the trumpet: praise Him with the psaltry and harp. ...praise Him with stringed instruments and organs. Praise Him upon the loud cymbals: praise Him upon the high sounding cymbals (Psalm 150:3-5).

Dance

Let them praise His name in the dance... (Psalm 149:3).

Praise Him with the timbrel and dance... (Psalm 150:4).

Let the children of Zion be joyful in their King (Psalm 149:2b).

This word *joyful*, or *gool* in Hebrew, as we examined earlier, is defined as "to spin around under the influence of any forcible, physical motion."

These are the basic four cornerstones concerning how to praise the Lord. *Singing* is an emotional expression and powerful connection as we come into agreement verbally with our God in praise and worship, boldly proclaiming His glory and majesty. *Musical instruments* set the stage and carry the power, presence, and mood of the Spirit through the air in a clearly understood language without words. *Dance* brings the fullness of surrender and humility through the expression of our physical bodies. When we use these elements to line up with and proclaim the *Word of God*, we greatly magnify, glorify, and exalt our God while doing powerfully effective damage to the enemy.

I'd like to point out that as we have been drawing our information from Psalms 149 and 150, Psalm 150 does not mention singing at all. This does not mean that singing was not a basic element in praise and worship, for we read in Psalm 149 that it certainly was. Not only did we read about it in Psalm 149, but we have seen it in other Scriptures as well.

There are many Scriptures that speak of praise but do not take the time to mention all four of these basic ingredients. In Psalms 149 and 150, dance is definitely one of the ingredients of praise according to God's Word. Therefore, when the praises of God's people are mentioned in Scripture, it is safe to assume that dance may very well have been a part of it, even if it does not mention the word *dance*.

As we studied King Jehoshaphat's victory, we saw that he sent out the singers and the praisers before the army. Does this mean that they did not use musical instruments, dance, or the Word of God just because these things were not specifically mentioned? No, in those days the praisers were those who sang, played musical instruments, and danced. Dance was a vitally functioning ingredient of praise and worship as God originally intended it to be. We the Church have been robbed of one of the basic foundational elements of our worship.

If one of the necessary elements of a thing is left out, the outcome or results of the final product will not be the fullness of what was originally intended. Let's say that you were going to bake some muffins, and the basic, necessary ingredients included flour, milk, eggs, and sugar. If you left out any one of these ingredients, the muffins would not be what you originally had in mind for the finished product. The results of the finished product that God originally intended for us in the fullness of praise and worship will not be experienced until dance is restored to its biblical order.

Keeping dance in mind as an ingredient, element, and factor of praise, let's take a look at the definitions of these words:

— *Ingredient*: something that enters into a compound or is a component part of any combination or mixture.

— *Element*: one of the factors determining the outcome of a process; a component, ingredient, factor. One of the parts of a compound or complex whole.

— *Factor*: any element whose presence helps activate; to perform a certain kind of work; to produce a definite result.

The dance was originally intended as a component that actively works together with singing, musical instruments, and the Word of God to produce, determine, and complete a certain outcome of definite results.

4. *Why*

The fourth building block of praise and worship can be broken down into four specific areas. *Why* should we praise the Lord? Consider the following four reasons taken from our two psalms:

1. *"For the Lord taketh pleasure"*

   Of all the reasons we are about to examine, my favorite is found in Psalm 149:4. This verse beautifully reveals the heart of God by stating, *"For the **Lord taketh pleasure in His people**...."* We are to praise God because it pleases Him. This truth has helped me many times to keep my focus on what God thinks as I have struggled with the judgments of man concerning my personal expression of praise to God in the dance. Regardless of what others' judgments may be, just knowing that my God takes great personal pleasure in me as I dance before Him has brought me great freedom.

2. *"His excellent greatness"*

   Praise Him for His mighty deeds; praise Him according to His excellent greatness (Psalm 150:2 NASB).

   Worthy art Thou, our Lord and our God, to receive glory and honor and power; for Thou didst create all things, and because of Thy will they existed, and were created (Revelation 4:11 NASB).

   ...Worthy is the Lamb that was slain to receive power and riches and wisdom and might and honor and glory and blessing (Revelation 5:12 NASB).

   He is the God of mighty deeds and excellent greatness! Not only is He the Creator of all things; He is the Lamb that was slain from the foundations of the earth. Why do we praise the Lord? *He alone is worthy to receive such praise!*

3. *"He will beautify the meek with salvation"*

   Our next point concerning why to praise God is also found in the second half of Psalm 149:4, *"He will beautify the meek with salvation."* As I shared in my testimony in the Introduction, it was the power of God's presence in praise and worship that broke the chains in my life that bound me and kept me from God.

As we look back to the example of Paul and Silas, we see that they not only found salvation from the bondage of shackles and prison through their praise, but the keeper of the prison and his whole house also received salvation that same night (see Acts 16:27-34). I have personally witnessed numerous times the salvation of the afflicted through the demonstration and ministry of the dance as the name of the Lord Jesus Christ was lifted up. Scripture tells us *"And I, if I be lifted up from the earth, will draw all men unto Me"* (John 12:32).

As we continue with the reasons for why we are to praise God, the puzzle pieces begin to come together. Now we have come to the part of this chapter that *hits the nail directly on the head* as we seek spiritual truth concerning dance as a spiritual weapon of war. Just as Jehoshaphat's army saw supernatural results as they obeyed God's direction in praise, we are about to examine the supernatural results available to us as we obey His Word by praising Him in the dance.

4. *"To execute vengeance upon the heathen"*

Verse 1 of Psalm 149 opens with a short sentence, saying, *"Praise ye the Lord."* The next five verses state *how*—with the Word of God, singing, musical instruments, and dance (see Ps. 149:2-6). The three verses following those tell us the *outcome, the definite, supernatural results* of our actions, as our praise powerfully and adversely affects the enemy:

To execute vengeance upon the heathen, and punishments upon the people; to bind their kings with chains, and their nobles with fetters of iron; to execute upon them the judgment written... (Psalm 149:7-9).

Vengeance is defined as "a warrantable retribution and punishment in support of the love of justice." In other words, it is justifiable payment, for our God is a just God. The word *execute* is also very important; it means "to perform it, to carry it to complete effect, to produce effect." Therefore, our praise performs and carries to complete effect the warrantable retribution of God's vengeance and punishment upon the enemy. *Praise God!*

An Effective Army

Years before I had discovered these truths in Psalm 149, God showed them to me in a different way. Back in 1983, when I first started out in the ministry of dance, I was very surprised at the powerful effect it had on the people. Their responses were far beyond complimentary. In fact, their reports had nothing whatsoever to do with complimenting me as a dancer. They spoke of Jesus and how He had touched, healed, and delivered them. One devout Catholic woman approached me after I had danced and told me she did not believe in all that "charismatic stuff." She then said, " But I want you to know, that was more than just a dance, there was something coming down off that platform." I'll never forget a very old Methodist woman who made her way up the center aisle with her walker after I danced. Approaching me, she tightly held both my hands, looked me straight in the eye, and simply said, "It was like a thousand prayers." Although these two women may not have known the charismatic words to express their feelings, they both knew what they had experienced was of God.

These were responses I had not expected. My spirit was full of questions as to why the dance had such a powerful effect on the people. As I sought the Lord for answers, I kept hearing the word *force* over and over in my spirit. God began to show me that it wasn't the dance itself that was so powerful, but it was the combination of its God-given attributes, together with the other powerful attributes of worship, which formed a *force* in the spirit realm.

In looking up the word *force*, I found some interesting definitions that led me to a deeper understanding of the spiritual power that was being manifest through the dance. Besides the more obvious definitions of the word *force*—such as strength, energy, and power—there were two definitions that clearly described this power I had been experiencing through the dance. The first was, "an army of soldiers." As the dance is executed, there is a *force*, or *army of soldiers* in the spirit, which make war in the heavenlies. I believe the angels, the heavenly host, play a very important part in this process of executing vengeance.

As we act in obedience to Psalm 149, praising the Lord with singing, musical instruments, dance, and the Word of God, there is a powerful release of the Word of God into the heavenlies. Scripture tells us that the angels, in turn, *perform* His Word; they hearken to and obey the voice of His Word. *"Bless the Lord, you His angels, mighty in strength, who perform His word, obeying the voice of His word!"* (Ps. 103:20 NASB). *Perform*, as it is used in this passage, is the same Hebrew word for execute that we examined in Psalm 149.

The second definition of the word *force* that I found most interesting is the word *efficacy*, meaning "power to produce effects." This word, *efficacy*, perfectly parallels our word *execute*, which we saw earlier means "to carry to complete effect, to perform, to produce effect." If we follow the instructions of Psalm 149 in spirit and in truth, we will see the results that the Scriptures promise. It's a package deal.

As we praise with singing, dancing, musical instruments, and the power of God's Word, an efficacy is activated as God's vengeance, punishment, and judgment are literally executed, performed, and carried to *complete effect* upon the enemy. Hallelujah!

What is this *complete effect*? Scripture tells us that it is the binding of their kings with chains and their nobles with fetters of iron (see Ps. 149:8). Remember, this is not a natural, physical battle we are speaking of, but a spiritual battle taking place in the supernatural realm. The spiritual rulers and powers that we fight against are clearly identified in the Book of Ephesians:

For we wrestle not against flesh and blood, but against principalities, against powers, against the rulers of the darkness of this world, against spiritual wickedness in high places (Ephesians 6:12).

At some place in our Christian walk, we must all come to terms with the fact that we are spiritual beings who are directly affected by spiritual matters. In the natural, we are helpless against these powers. Shooting a gun into the heavenlies or frantically punching our fists into the air has no effect whatsoever against supernatural powers, but God has equipped us with mighty and powerful spiritual weapons of war designed to successfully pull down these strongholds. Dance is one of these weapons.

For though we walk in the flesh, we do not war against the flesh: (For the weapons of our warfare are not carnal, but mighty through God, to the pulling down of strong holds) (2 Corinthians 10:3-4).

I have seen the demonstration of God's Spirit and power countless times in the pulling down of strongholds through the spiritual weapon of war we call dance. To those who have never experienced dance in this way it may seem to be as far-fetched as what took place with Jehoshaphat's army or in the falling of the walls of Jericho. But, just as those things truly happened, so the gift of dance is a true spiritual weapon and a key to seeing God's power manifested in what may appear to be unlikely measures.

Spiritual Strongholds and Dance

One way that dance specifically works to defeat the enemy is by tearing down spiritual *strongholds*. Any area of your life upon which satan has a strong grip or hold is a stronghold. A stronghold can be in the area of fear, anger, lust, adultery, bad habits, or bitterness. It can also be in the area of addiction to something like drugs, alcohol, or nicotine. A stronghold is exactly what the word appears to be: It is anything that holds on so strong that it is not easily shaken or changed. To live victoriously, the believer must tear down every stronghold of satan in his or her life.

However, there are two sides to the concept of a stronghold. A "stronghold" is not necessarily a bad thing; it all depends upon the context of the word. For example, if I had just slipped and fallen over a steep mountain ledge, catching myself on a branch that momentarily held me between life and death, I would want someone who had a very strong hold to reach over the edge to rescue me. I would also put forth every ounce of my own strength to take a very strong hold of that lifeline between me and death.

This should be the position of Christ in our life. He has saved us from certain death. Therefore, I want to walk through my life having a very *strong hold* on God, knowing that when troubles come my way I am safe and secure in His strength. For He is my refuge and my strength (see Ps 46:1). The word *refuge* is one of the Greek definitions for the word *stronghold*. When we hold strongly onto Him, He holds strongly onto us. In Him, we find safety, protection, and a refuge from our enemies so that we may walk securely in the things of God.

Although there are two sides to the spiritual power of a stronghold, the basic definition holds true for both, whether to the good or evil. A stronghold, once again, is anything that has a tight grip upon us and is not easily shaken or changed. It is a powerful spiritual force. And, just as there are two sides to the power of a stronghold, there are also two sides to the spiritual power of the dance in relation to that stronghold. The four basic elements of praise can be used to powerfully and effectively pull down the spiritual strongholds of the enemy. However, we must be aware that these same elements can also be used by the enemy to loosen and pull down our stronghold in God.

Because dance is such a natural instinct within us, it is far too easy to enter into agreement with the compelling force of the world's music and dance without realizing the danger to which we are opening ourselves up in the spirit realm. Time after time, worldly dance has been a strong and powerfully deceptive force in loosening the grip of God's stronghold while tightening the grip of satan's.

For God or the Enemy?

When we as Christians express ourselves in some form of dance by taking the precious holy instruments of our bodies, which God created and entrusted to us for worship, and use them to come into agreement with the world, reflecting and promoting its sinful, carnal nature, we defile ourselves. Whether we realize it or not, by coming into this form of agreement, we are literally joining forces with the opposite side. Many Christians are unaware of this danger, and many have been deceived into believing that singing secular songs or dancing to secular music is relatively harmless. However, few things can tear down our stronghold in God more quickly.

Just as we can see the *definite results* of tearing down satan's work through complete surrender to God in worship through singing, music, dance, and the Word of God, we can also witness *definite results* from tearing down God's stronghold in our lives by surrendering ourselves and coming into agreement with singing, music, dance, and the words of the enemy.

Words

Words are powerful, and many songs sing the same thing over and over—driving the message deep into our spirits. The words of a worship song can build up our spirit in godliness. However, worldly lyrics can stir up and promote our carnal nature, tearing down our stronghold in God. Either way, the singing of words has a powerful effect on our spirits.

Music

The words are not the only component in this force; when the power of music accompanies and joins with the words, they become a very compelling force. Music has an unmatched ability to instantaneously move the emotions of man. Music can be an audible manifestation of man's emotion, and it has a miraculous power to affect the spirit, soul, and body of man. Music was created to stimulate the emotions, and it works. Music can powerfully stimulate every emotion known to man. And when you touch the emotions of a person, you literally open the door to his soul, reaching far beyond that person's intellect. It is a dangerous thing for anyone to willingly open his soul and come into agreement with the powerful influences of ungodly, worldly music and its words.

Singing

We proceed to add fuel to this danger when we come into a verbal, audible agreement with these words by singing along. At this point, the compelling power of the words and music have motivated us to the point of some level of physical response. In this case, singing is an instinctive, seemingly harmless response. Although this is an instinctive response, it is not harmless. By surrendering ourselves to the point of cooperation and agreement by singing along, we further open the door of our souls to these powerful influences.

These three avenues of expression—the power of singing, the power of the music, and the power of the words in the music—affect the spirit and soul of man, but the complete effect does not come into play until the third part of our being joins with the expression. It is actually impossible to move the spirit and soul without having an effect on the body, for they are one. The physical body releases and demonstrates the emotions that have been stimulated by the music and singing. That demonstration may be as simple as tapping your foot, bouncing your knee, drumming your hand on the table, clapping, or even swaying to the music. These are all forms of dance. In each case, we are physically coming into agreement with our emotions and beginning to move to the message of the music. It is only natural for man to have this release; it is the way God created us.

The fact that this force is so instinctive in man is undeniable, but why did God make us this way? As instruments of emotional expression, our bodies were created for the purpose of enabling us to enter into a personal, intimate experience of worship and relationship with God that affects us entirely— spirit, soul, and body—and allows us to become one with our God. As long as we live in these physical bodies, the fullness of our worship is not complete without the expression of our physical bodies, for they are a part of our whole being.

This is what makes dance the element of our praise and worship that completes the fullness of our surrender and produces satisfaction, not only in us, but also to God. When we enter into this level of agreement, surrendering our entire being in worship to God, we increase His embrace and stronghold in us. It is frightening to realize that these same principles can also be powerfully effective to produce negative results in us when we come into agreement with satan's kingdom through singing and dancing to words and music that reflect the character and nature of this world.

The Key of Obedience

And having in a readiness to revenge all disobedience, when your obedience is fulfilled (2 Corinthians 10:6).

The key idea here is the concept of "fulfilled obedience." Can we trust in God's Word concerning praise and worship to the degree of acting in obedience to it, even if it doesn't make sense to our fleshly, carnal nature? The enemy has deceived us into believing lies about the dance that directly oppose what the Word of God tells us is true. Rather than follow the enemy's lies, we need to follow these directions Paul wrote in a previous verse, "*...refute arguments and theories and reasonings and every proud and lofty thing that sets itself up against the* [true] *knowledge of God...*" (2 Cor. 10:5 AMP).

No wonder satan has worked so desperately and relentlessly to keep the truth of dance from us. He knows once we act in full obedience that all disobedience is revenged or punished; he becomes bound as spiritual strongholds are pulled down. Our obedience and surrender to God is freedom for us and bondage to satan. It is bad enough for satan that the judgment against him has been written, but for us to discover what executes and activates that judgment is his greatest nightmare.

The key is obedience. Yes, as difficult as it may be for the Body of Christ at large to accept, the truth is that dance is a powerful spiritual weapon of war, and it is *"mighty through God to the pulling down of strong holds"* (2 Cor. 10:4).

This does not mean that everyone has to dance or be part of a public performance or expression; that would be ridiculous. That would be like saying that everyone has to play a musical instrument. But the Scripture says, *"Let them praise His name in the dance"* (Ps. 149:3a). It does not say, "stop them," nor does it say, "force them." It specifically says, "let them." My dear friend Judson Cornwall once explained to me, "'Let them' is more than permission granted; it is the word of a king that commands. When God said, 'Let there be light,' it was not permission for illumination; it was a creative command. When God says, 'Let them praise Him in the dance,' it is a creative command; nothing can stop it. Hallelujah."

It is important that the element of dance exist as part of our praise and worship as God has commanded. When its force is joined with the other elements, our worship will produce the full effect of God's original intent and purpose. Dance is a powerful tool designed to affect the overall outcome of the power and authority God has entrusted to His people for spiritual warfare. I pray that we as the Church by the grace of God will come into the true understanding and function of dance in spiritual warfare. Otherwise, we will continue to carry around a powerful weapon that is of no use to us, and the enemy will continue to use the elements of music, singing, and dance against us like a pied piper, leading the saints of God and our children down the path to hell.

CHAPTER 11

~

Beautiful Feet
(Proclaiming the Good Tidings)

How beautiful upon the mountains are the feet of him that bringeth good tidings, that publisheth peace; that bringeth good tidings of good, that publisheth salvation; that saith unto Zion, Thy God reigneth! (Isaiah 52:7).

Our feet and their use as a spiritual type must not be overlooked as we seek God's fullness in the restoration of dance. Remembering that there is no clear-cut line separating what is and what is not dance, the use of our feet in the dance covers anything from walking in a processional to twirling, marching, skipping, stomping, etc. God says that our feet are beautiful when they are used to bring forth and publish the good tidings of salvation.

This word *publisheth* is a Hebrew word meaning "to cause to tell; declare; cause to, let, or make to hear; proclaim; proclamation; report; show forth." When we dance, we not only tell, declare, proclaim, and report, but we show forth the good tidings though the physical demonstration and communication of our body language. Spiritually, this is a powerful proclamation, for it encompasses all that is within us, spirit, soul, and body.

Dance Your Dances, O Judah

Behold, on the mountains the feet of him who brings good news, who announces peace! Celebrate your feasts, O Judah; pay your vows. For never again will the wicked one pass through you; He is cut off completely (Nahum 1:15 NASB).

Again we see the demonstration of bringing forth the good news and announcing peace through the use of our feet.

The word *celebrate*, as found in this reference, is the Hebrew word *chagag*, meaning "to move in a circle, to march in a sacred processional; to observe a festival; to be giddy; to celebrate; *to dance*; to keep hold a solemn feast; to reel to and fro." This is how the Jewish people kept the feasts of the Lord. They danced, celebrated, and had sacred processionals. As we read this same Scripture in the King James Version, instead of saying "*celebrate* your feasts," it says, "*keep* thy solemn feasts." *Celebrate* and *keep* are both translated from the same Hebrew word, *chagag*.

Who would have thought that the word *keep* would mean to dance! Dance was such an integral part of how the Israelites celebrated the feasts that to *keep* a feast literally refers to marching, reeling to and fro, and celebrating in the dance. Seven different times in the Scripture the word *chagag* is translated as *keep*. Not only is that interesting, but the word *feasts* (as in, "*celebrate your feasts*") that is used in this verse is also translated from the word, *chagag*. Therefore, we could read Nahum 1:15 as saying, "Not only celebrate, or keep your feasts, O Judah, but dance your dances."

It is also quite interesting and fitting to note that the name *Judah* is translated from the Hebrew language as *praise*. Therefore this verse could also quite appropriately read, "Dance your dances, oh praisers"! Hallelujah! May the praise dancers of God declare, publish, and show forth the good news through the use of their "beautiful feet."

Let His Enemies Be Scattered

Let God arise, let His enemies be scattered; and let those who hate Him flee before Him. As smoke is driven away, so drive them away; as wax melts before the fire, so let the wicked perish before God (Psalm 68:1-2 NASB).

These strong words speak not only of warfare, but of victory over the enemy. What was taking place in the natural to release such power, causing the enemy to scatter, flee, and melt like wax before fire? Verses 11 and 12, of this same chapter say,

The Lord gives the command; the women who proclaim the good tidings are a great host: kings of armies flee, they flee... (Psalm 68:11-12 NASB).

Praise God! Again we see the proclaiming of good tidings. This particular Scripture specifies that they are women and that they are a *great army* that causes kings of armies to flee!

As we continue, we see that verse 24 of this psalm speaks of a great processional into the sanctuary. Again we see the maidens, and this time it specifies that they have tambourines.

They have seen Thy procession, O God, the procession of my God, my King, into the sanctuary. The singers went on, the musicians after them, in the midst of the maidens beating tambourines (Psalm 68:24-25 NASB).

These women didn't walk along solemnly dragging their feet and beating their tambourines. No, they danced and rejoiced with gladness as they proclaimed the good news. It was powerful, effective warfare that caused kings of armies to flee. And God's Word says, *"How beautiful are their feet."*

The word *midst* is used to describe where the women were dancing. It is the Hebrew word *tavek*, meaning "the center, between, in the middle, among." This suggests that the dancers were not hidden in the back somewhere, but they were right in the middle or center of the action of proclaiming praise to the Lord in His sanctuary.

What has happened to damage, even eliminate, these great and powerful processionals in the sanctuary of God? Psalm 74:3-4 (NASB) tells us, "...*The enemy has damaged everything within the sanctuary. Thine adversaries have roared in the midst of Thy meeting place; they have set up their own standards for signs.*"

Do not be deceived by any standards that the enemy may set up in the sanctuary in the name of so-called decency, order, or tradition. As I said in my testimony at the beginning of this book, through the traditions of my church I was taught to sit still and be quiet; for quietness meant holiness, and this stillness equated good and acceptable behavior before God. Yes, there is a time to be quiet before the Lord, but if all we ever did was keep still, we would be disobeying God's instructions for how He desires to be glorified in His sanctuary. However, the sanctuary is not a building of brick and stone, but we as living stones are the sanctuary, the temple of the Holy Spirit (see 1 Cor. 3:16; 1 Pet. 2:5). We must celebrate our God in the sanctuary, and "dance your dances, O Judah."

The direct connection between victory and the use of our feet as a spiritual type is found throughout Scripture.

> ...*But I want you to be wise in what is good, and innocent in what is evil. And the God of peace will soon crush Satan* **under your feet** (Romans 16:19-20 NASB).

> *Every place on which* **the sole of your foot treads,** *I have given it to you, just as I spoke to Moses* (Joshua 1:3 NASB).

> *And when those who carried the ark came to the Jordan,* **and the feet of the priests** *carrying the ark were dipped in the edge of the water (for the Jordan overflows all its banks all the days of harvest), that the waters which were flowing down from above stood up and rose up in one heap...* (Joshua 3:15-16 NASB).

*And it came about when the priests who carried the ark of the covenant of the Lord had come up from the middle of the Jordan, and the **soles of the priests' feet** were lifted up to the dry ground, that the waters of the Jordan returned to their place, and went over all its banks as before* (Joshua 4:18 NASB).

*I pursued my enemies and destroyed them, and I did not turn back until they were consumed. And I have devoured them and shattered them, so that they did not rise; and they fell **under my feet*** (2 Samuel 22:38-39 NASB).

*Thou madest him to have dominion over the works of Thy hands; Thou hast put all things **under his feet*** (Psalm 8:6).

*O clap your hands, all peoples; shout to God with the voice of joy. For the Lord Most High is to be feared, a great King over all the earth. He subdues peoples under us, and nations **under our feet*** (Psalm 47:1-3 NASB).

*Give us help from trouble: for vain is the help of man. Through God we shall do valiantly: for He it is that shall **tread down** our enemies* (Psalm 108:12-13).

*Behold, I give unto you power to **tread** on serpents and scorpions, and over all the power of the enemy: and nothing shall by any means hurt you* (Luke 10:19).

*And it came about when they brought these kings out to Joshua, that Joshua called for all the men of Israel, and said to the chiefs of the men of war who had gone with him, "Come near, put your **feet on the necks** of these kings." So they came near, and they put **their feet on their necks.** Joshua then said to them, "Do not fear or be dismayed! Be strong and courageous, for thus the Lord will do to all your enemies with whom you fight"* (Joshua 10:24-25 NASB).

Remember, it is the serpent as a type of satan who has been cursed by God with no feet with which to walk upright. Scripture says, *"...upon thy belly shalt thou go..."* (Gen. 3:14). This places us in a good position to put our foot upon satan's neck (which seems to be the proper way to stop a serpent). If you step on the tail of a serpent, he can turn around and bite you. Maybe this is why the Word of God provides us with this type of putting our foot on the necks of our enemies.

"Give Me Back My Slippers"

These are exciting truths regarding our feet as powerful spiritual weapons. God is beginning to open the eyes of the Church in order to reveal the hidden treasures of His original intent and purpose for the dance. It is as though we are waking up, looking down, and finding these powerful shoes called *dance* upon our feet. One of satan's greatest fears is that we will receive revelation of these truths and begin to fully operate in them. This is why he is doing his best to discredit the function of dance in the church. Now that the Church is becoming aware of this gift, he is working hard to convince its members that dance belongs to him and was created for his own carnal, sinful purposes.

One night I was watching the movie, *The Wizard of Oz,* with my son Jacob when I began to see several descriptive parallels between the story of Dorothy, the witch, and the ruby slippers with the position of dance in the church and the schemes of the enemy. If you remember, the Wicked Witch of the West wanted the ruby slippers off Dorothy's feet. In anger and desperation, she addressed Dorothy, saying, "Give me back my slippers. I'm the only one who knows how to use them; they are of no use to you. Give them back to me, give them back!"

But Glenda, the good witch, gave sound advice to Dorothy saying, "Keep tight inside of them. Their magic must be very powerful, or she wouldn't want them so badly." Like the ruby slippers on Dorothy's feet that were full of power she didn't know how to use, so the Church is awakening to the spiritual power and authority of the dance as an effective tool, not only in praise and worship, but also in warfare.

As Dorothy stood there bewildered, not really understanding what was going on, Glenda pointed to Dorothy's feet, and addressing the wicked witch said, "It's too late. There they are, and there they'll stay." Then she said to Dorothy, "I'm afraid you've made a rather bad enemy of the Wicked Witch of the West." No kidding! Anyone who has attempted to pioneer in the restoration of dance can testify that they have indeed confronted "a rather bad enemy."

This reminds me of the apostle Paul as he states in First Corinthians 16:9, *"For a wide door for effective service has opened to me, and there are many adversaries."*

Just like the Church and dance, Dorothy never asked for the ruby slippers, and she wasn't even sure she wanted them. She just looked down, and there they were on her feet. As the wicked witch stated, "I'm the only one that knows how to use them; they are of no use to you," the Church, like Dorothy, has found itself standing in shoes full of power that they don't know how to use. Just like the advice Glenda gave to Dorothy was, "Stay tight inside them," my advice to the Church is, "Stay inside them!" The shoes of dance must be very powerful or the enemy wouldn't want them so badly.

If you remember, the witch followed hard after Dorothy and her friends with the driving purpose of getting those shoes off Dorothy's feet. When the trial got intense, Dorothy wanted to give up the shoes immediately. Dorothy did not really understand the power of the ruby slippers any more than the Church understands the power of the dance. This parallels the Church and its attempt to function in the dance with minimal understanding, wanting to disregard its function at the first signs of trouble.

Because of a lack of knowledge, even those with the best intentions find themselves unequipped to withstand the degree of warfare that is inevitable in repossessing this gift from the camp of the enemy.

In the Church we have those who are passionately in favor of the dance, those who are passionately against it, and those who believe that the level of division over this seemingly optional issue is *just not worth it*. It is no wonder that so many who have bravely stepped out to pioneer in this area have eventually aborted their mission.

The enemy knew this day of restoration would come long before the idea of dance became an issue in the contemporary Church. Although his traps are pre-calculated and well-laid, the Word of God is anointed to expose every scheme and undo every strategy, and to bring a new level of freedom, power, and authority in our worship through the truth. As I said before, one of satan's greatest fears is that we will receive revelation of these truths and begin successfully operating in them.

In Psalm 74:4 (NASB), we see that our adversary has *"roared in the midst of* [God's] *meeting place."* It is now time for the Lion of Judah to roar in our meeting places, bringing the prophetic word of truth and proclaiming the good tidings of peace as we dance our dances, treading on the neck of our enemy. Let us tell, declare, proclaim, report, and show forth the gospel of peace through the use of our feet, for we are a great army. Kings of armies flee—they flee! So dance your dances, O Judah, using the powerful weapon of war we call dance, for *how beautiful are your feet!*

CHAPTER 12

~

Order in the Restoration

As worship is being restored in the Church, the desire of my heart is that we would ascend into dimensions of communion far beyond what we ever imagined possible. These are exciting words, and all those who love God wholeheartedly "amen" such a statement. The problem with all this desire and excitement is that we far too often lack the proper wisdom concerning God's order in the restoration process.

It is impossible for us to come into the fullness of what was originally intended for the dance if we do not seek after God's biblical order. Biblical order does not always include what we think seems orderly, but it is exclusive to God's will as He has instructed in His Word. The biblical order of worship is very serious business with God as we are about to witness in the next scriptural example of Moses' nephews, Nadab and Abihu.

And Nadab and Abihu, the sons of Aaron, each took his censer and put fire in it, and put incense on it, and offered strange and unholy fire before the Lord, as He had not commanded them. And there came forth fire from before the Lord and killed them, and they died before the Lord. Then Moses said to Aaron, This is what the Lord meant when He said, I [and My will, not their own] will be acknowledged as hallowed by those who come near Me, and before all the people I will be honored. And Aaron said nothing (Leviticus 10:1-3 AMP).

A key line in this Scripture is, *"I [and My will, not their own] will be acknowledged as hallowed by those who come near Me...."* Many of us desire to be of those who truly come near the Lord in worship, but this can only be accomplished according to the order of God's will, and never our own. Nadab and Abihu were of a high order in the priesthood, which allowed them to be of those permitted to come near to the Lord with their offering of worship. Today, because of the shed blood of Jesus, we have all become priests who are allowed to *"come boldly unto the throne of grace"* (Heb. 4:16).

Praise God! He has provided a way for us to come near Him, but we must realize that God's holiness has not changed, and the words of Leviticus 10:3 (AMP) still hold true, *"I [and My will, not their own] will be acknowledged as hallowed by those who come near Me."* I believe much of the worship existing in the Church today is not acknowledged as hallowed, for it is not according to what God instructed; it is more in line with what seems right to a man.

There is a way which seemeth right unto a man, but the end thereof are the ways of death (Proverbs 14:12).

The last two Scriptures we examined spoke of how our own ways result in death. Obviously, this does not mean that if we worship according to man's traditions versus the biblical order of God that we will be struck dead as Nadab and Abihu were. I believe that as we apply the principle of this story to our worship today, it is more of a guideline to what is effective and full of life versus what is ineffective and lifeless.

It is not for me to judge the worship of any man's heart; that is an intimate, personal matter between man and God. I only know from experience that the ways in which God has instructed us to worship Him are effective. It only makes sense that if God knows the make-up of man—spirit, soul, and body—and if He has created man for worship, then the ways that He has instructed us to worship Him would be designed to best accomplish this purpose.

I understand that the transition from traditional worship to the more outward, biblical expressions can be difficult and uncomfortable at first. It is humbling to lift your hands, kneel, bow, or outwardly express the innermost feelings of your heart. I believe humility is a key ingredient in true worship and God has instructed us to openly express ourselves for this reason. I pray in these last days that a deep hunger for the presence of God will literally invade the Church to such a degree that we will all remove any and every hindrance that would prevent us from fulfilling that desire.

For the most part, this responsibility lies in the hands of the leadership. You might be surprised at how quickly the people will respond to new expressions of worship as they are introduced with the support of Scripture and a heart that clearly reflects a desire to please God. It's not that these people do not love God; it is that they have never been taught how to worship or perhaps allowed to worship according to God's original instructions.

The last portion of Leviticus 10:3 (AMP) says, "*...and before all the people I will be honored....*" The word *honored* sticks out to me here. If I were to honor my husband with a special birthday dinner, I would fix his favorite foods prepared the way he likes them. For example, if I were to make him a carrot cake for dessert, knowing that his favorite cake is chocolate, I would not be honoring him. Personally, I may like carrot cake much better than chocolate cake, but it is my *husband* whom I am focusing on to please and honor with this special birthday dinner, not myself. Similarly, we are missing the significance of honor in true worship when our offering is limited to what we are comfortable with and have personally decided is acceptable for God.

For My thoughts are not your thoughts, neither are your ways My ways, saith the Lord. For as the heavens are higher than the earth, so are My ways higher than your ways, and My thoughts than your thoughts (Isaiah 55:8-9).

There is no doubt that the revelation of dance has hit the Church and is in the process of being restored. It is the order of that process that is vital to the success of the restoration, and, until we understand this point, we will continue to fall short.

A Strong Foundation

The order of the restoration of dance is much like that of building a house. When my husband was building our home, I was amazed at the numerous unseen things that had to be done before the final, rewarding stages came into view. The house had to be constructed in a meticulous and very specific order. I remember feeling frustrated and even bored with having to wait for unseen things to be finished. I wasn't too excited about things like the foundation, wiring, and plumbing. From the very beginning, I was ready to pick out carpeting, hang wallpaper, and move in. By witnessing the whole process, I gained a whole new respect for the wisdom and patience of carpentry. Building in order is definitely a vital necessity.

I thought building a new house from scratch was a lot of work, but ask anyone who builds, and he will tell you that it is even more work to restore a damaged old house than to build a new one from scratch. This has a definite parallel to the restoration of dance. For the dance is not new; it is as old as creation, and it has definitely been severely damaged. The foundation of our understanding of the dance has been laid crooked. The Church has as many deceptions and perversions to tear down, as it has walls of truth and purity to rebuild.

Scripture tells us to be anxious for nothing, but it seems that the Body of Christ is in a hurry when it comes to the dance, wanting to pick out carpeting and hang wallpaper at a time when we should be concerned with laying a deep, strong foundation. This is why we have seen many so-called dance ministries come quickly onto the scene only to crash and burn. Good intentions are not enough. Many have attempted to touch God's purpose for dance only to sadly watch it perish in their church for lack of knowledge (see Hos. 4:6). Yet we do not lack knowledge concerning the dance because God has withheld it. Rather, we lack knowledge because we have not sought Him for it. It's all in the Book.

> *All scripture is given by inspiration of God, and is profitable for doctrine, for reproof, for correction, for instruction in righteousness* (2 Timothy 3:16).

As our biblical forefathers set both good and bad examples for us, we can receive instruction in righteousness from them and wisely learn from their mistakes. Without adherence to these biblical truths, we will most assuredly and miserably fail.

When I first started out in the ministry of dance in 1983, I was no different than many of those who are struggling today. I too was perishing for lack of knowledge. I had only a small piece of the puzzle, and I was attempting to run with it. Although my motives were pure, my zeal was great, and I had only the best of intentions, I handled the holiness of God in ignorance. If I had continued in this way without seeking, obtaining, and obeying God's order, I am sure that I would not be in this ministry today.

Our Way vs. God's Way

First Chronicles 13-15 provides an illustration of the seriousness of God's **due order**. In chapter 13, we see King David consulting with his captains and with every leader, saying, *"...If it seem good unto you, and that it be of the Lord our God...let us bring again the ark of our God to us..."* (1 Chron. 13:2-3).

The ark of the covenant was a wooden box covered in gold. It contained the tablets on which the Ten Commandments were inscribed, Aaron's rod that budded, and a jar of manna from the wilderness. There is a great deal of rich and beautiful teaching concerning the ark and its significance that we will not go into here. The important thing to understand in reference to this teaching is that at that time the very manifest presence of God dwelt in the ark, and the ark was holy.

God's Word had clearly instructed that no man was to touch the ark. Anyone who did so would die. Only the Levites were allowed to transport the ark, and then only by slipping long poles, or staves, through gold rings attached to its sides. They were to support the poles on their shoulders as they walked. Now David wanted to restore the ark of God's presence to the midst of the people. Not only was this a good idea; it was a God idea, and everyone was very excited.

In First Chronicles 13:7, we see that the people were transporting the ark of God, not by staves on the shoulders of Levites, but on a new cart. Two men named Uzza and Ahio were driving the cart. King David and all Israel rejoiced before God with all their might singing and playing harps, psalteries, tambourines, cymbals, and trumpets. It must have been quite an emotionally exciting day—that is, until they came to the threshing floor of Chidon. At the threshing floor, the oxen stumbled, the ark tipped, and Uzza put forth his hand to hold it steady. As a result, the following happened:

> *And the anger of the Lord was kindled against Uzza, and He smote him, because he put his hand to the ark: and there he died before God. And David was displeased, because the Lord had made a breach upon Uzza: wherefore that place is called Perezuzza to this day. And David was afraid of God that day, saying, How shall I bring the ark of God home to me? So David brought not the ark home to himself to the city of David, but carried it aside into the house of Obede-dom the Gittite* (1 Chronicles 13:10-13).

I'm sure the music, rejoicing, and celebration were replaced with a solemn fear of God as the people carefully took the ark aside to the house of Obededom that day, where it remained for the next three months.

Let's stop and parallel this passage to the restoration of dance. King David and all Israel thought it was a good idea to restore the presence of God to the people. Similarly, there is also a move sweeping the Church today that is full of excitement and assured by the Spirit of God that it is God's will and pleasure for dance to be restored in holiness to His people. What happened in this passage is an important warning for those who have been entrusted as leaders in the dance: King David and all Israel proceeded to do the right thing (restoring the ark), but they did it in the *wrong way* by transporting it on a cart rather than carrying it by staves on the Levites' shoulders as God had commanded. The ark was holy and was not to be touched by the arm of the flesh. Likewise, the dance is holy before God and is not to be touched by the arm of the flesh.

Being overly excited and emotional can be dangerous if it causes you to move out in the flesh. God will not allow His holiness to be treated with irreverence—whether consciously or unconsciously. Sooner or later the matter will come to the threshing floor and will be threshed. Those who have proceeded in the actions of the restoration of dance with no regard for its holiness to God will sooner or later be threshed. The presence of God that is manifest in the dance will not be restored as long as man attempts to restore it in the flesh.

When the ark began to tip due to the stumbling of the oxen, a man of good intention put out his hand to steady it, and he was instantly struck dead. Interestingly enough, this man's name was Uzza. The Hebrew definition of the name *Uzza* is "strength." Man cannot attempt to touch, hold up, transport, or restore the holiness of God in his own strength. What did Uzza put to the ark? It was his *hand*. This word is another Hebrew word indicating power, means, and direction. Uzza, symbolizing man's strength, attempted to touch the holiness of God with his own power, means, and direction. He suffered the consequences of acting contrary to God's direction and acting out of his own strength and reasoning.

The Responsibility of Leadership

If David, the leadership, would have sought God in the first place and obeyed His original order, the ark would have been on staves and would never have been in danger of falling. There would have been no oxen to stumble. Therefore, Uzza would not have been killed for trying to steady the ark. This is a strong warning for the leadership of God. Leading and directing others according to God's order is their responsibility. This casualty was the responsibility of the leader, King David, because he failed to adhere to the blueprints of God's **due order**.

If my child, for lack of knowledge, reaches up and touches a hot burner on the stove, he will surely be burned. The fact that he doesn't understand the danger does not protect him from the consequences. As his parent, it is my responsibility to teach him not to touch the stove until he is mature enough to handle it in an appropriate manner.

Just as David in his excitement attempted to do the right thing in the wrong way, so is this level of excitement causing some churches to fall into the same error. Like Uzza, who was a type of touching what is holy in his own strength, these churches have taken the dance, which is holy to God, into their own hands, presenting lifeless demonstrations that are detrimental to the orderly restoration of dance.

One afternoon at a worship conference in Detroit, I was having a conversation regarding dance with a well-known worship leader. He travels extensively and is quite current with what is happening in worship throughout the Church today. He told me that there was a time when there was literally an explosion in dance. Everywhere he went there was dancing and dance presentations, but then suddenly it all seemed to stop. He said that he didn't understand why this happened. I believe what has happened is that the Church has basically attempted to restore the dance on a man-made cart. Because of this error, we have seen many lifeless dances, and the dance is now at the threshing floor. Praise God! Just as King David stopped everything and took the time to seek God's direction in His Word, so must we.

Prepare the Way

In First Chronicles 15:1, we find David taking a different approach. Here we see that he prepared a place for the ark of God, including pitching a tent for it. To me, this speaks of the need for proper preparation in the restoration. Each church needs to take the time to present sound preparatory teaching concerning the dance so that it may be fully restored to God's glory, honor, and power.

David also affirmed God's order for proper transportation of the ark: "*...None ought to carry the ark of God but the Levites: for them hath the Lord chosen to carry the ark of God...*" (1 Chron. 15:2). Likewise, there are those who have been specifically called to the ministry of dance in the Church. Like the Levites, these dance ministers will transport and carry upon their shoulders the manifest presence of God. This ministry is not to be touched by those who are not specifically called, or it will produce only death in this ministry.

The next thing David did was gather all the Levitical leadership and say to them,

> *...Ye are the chief of the fathers of the Levites: sanctify your-selves, both ye and your brethren, that ye may bring up the ark of the Lord God of Israel unto the place that I have prepared for it. For because ye did it not at the first, the Lord our God made a breach upon us, for that we sought Him not after the due order* (1 Chronicles 15:12-13).

David knew that their failure was directly connected with not fol-lowing God's due order. In the fear of God, he now instructed all the leaders to **sanctify themselves**, knowing that God's presence could only be restored in purity. This holy procedure was not to be altered by the good intentions of man or tainted by the ways of the world. When Uzza put forth his hand to steady the ark, I am sure it was with only the best of intentions. But for a lack of knowledge, he perished (see Hos. 4:6).

Scripture also tells us in Second Samuel 6:7 that it was because of Uzza's error, rashness, and irreverence that he was struck down. I believe this was due to his lack of knowledge, which resulted in a lack of respect for the holiness of God. One of our greatest hindrances in the restoration of dance parallels this same lack of knowledge concerning the holiness God originally intended for dance.

The precious gift of dance cannot be restored in the midst of error, rashness, and irreverence. Yet we see all three of these off-centered extremes taking place in the Church. We have leadership that refuses to allow the Church to have anything to do with dance (this is error due to lack of knowledge), and we have leadership who allow the people to leap before they look (this is rash and irreverent again, due to a lack of knowledge). Either way, God's order is lost and satan's strategy succeeds. In a nutshell, if satan cannot beat the Church out of the dance, he will join the Church in the dance. We must be wise to his ways to discern and disarm his plan. If we lack this wisdom, we create a perfect seedbed for satan's tares to be sown alongside of, if not in place of, the wheat.

Although godly dance has suffered violent assault and at one point almost completely vanished, satan's original plan to completely steal dance away from the Church has entirely failed. It's too late; the idea that **dance is God's will** has been released as a glorious revelation to the Church, and it is growing quickly.

Order Brings Life

Although in many cases this revelation concerning the dance is still in seed form, I believe that we can appropriately compare the restoration of dance to the gestation and birth of a baby. From the time of her birth, each female has within her all the seeds, or eggs, she will ever use to reproduce or give birth to another life. Yet, it is not until a particular stage of maturity that one of those seeds can be fertilized and begin to produce new life. As the Church has matured, the time has come for this seed to begin to grow and produce life.

Every congregation has its own gestation period. Some are excited about the pregnancy, while others are experiencing more of an unwanted pregnancy. The enemy's strategy is to bring an abortion to this pregnancy before there is birth and new life. Some churches are faithfully holding on for dear life, while others are more than willing to abort this life to relieve themselves of the responsibilities and difficulties attached with this pregnancy.

To those who have given birth and are already experiencing the joys and trials of the early months and years of the dance, always hold the dance in a hand that is wide open and submissive to the moving of the Spirit. *Never* grip it or take it into your own control. Continually allow God to go before you as your defense. Never attempt to force or make your own way. Believe me, He is faithful and true and can move mountains if you stay out of His way.

To those who anxiously await the birth, beware of rushing the gestation. Babies who are born prematurely are often unhealthy, and sometimes they even die. To those who are experiencing an unwanted pregnancy and want to let go of the entire concept, my advice to you is, instead of focusing on your doubts, suspicions, and fears, hold on tight. Go directly to the Father and seek His heart in this matter through prayer and study of His Word.

As I stated in the Introduction of this book, we are most assuredly living in the period of the restoration of all things (see Acts 3:21). Things are moving quickly in the physical world, as well as in the spiritual realm of the Kingdom of God. The Book of Daniel says of these days that *"...many shall run to and fro, and knowledge shall be increased"* (Dan. 12:4). The prophet Haggai says, *"The glory of this latter house shall be greater than of the former..."* (Hag. 2:9). And Habakkuk says, *"For the earth shall be filled with the knowledge of the glory of the Lord, as the waters cover the sea"* (Hab. 2:14).

In the true restoration of dance to the glory of the latter house, it is important that our knowledge be increased, not only in how and why the dance was lost but also in how and why it must be revealed and restored. We must also be cautious not to exalt it in such a way that it becomes something more than or other than what God intended. Yet we must also desire to see the hidden treasures of this precious gift functioning in the fullness for which it was created.

As the trial on dance proceeds, it should be in the heart of every Christian juror for the final verdict to be nothing less than the full declaration of truth. This truth will only be found as we humbly submit, willingly surrendering ourselves, to God in obedience to His commandments and in accordance with the due order of His will. In remembrance of Leviticus 10:3 (AMP), "...*I [and My will, not their own] will be acknowledged as hallowed by those who come near Me...*," may we, in fear and humility, desire God's will—nothing more, nothing less, nothing else.

Let's take the time to get the foundation straight and be wise workers, not to be found working in vain and in ignorance against God in this restoration process. For our God is the Lord of the dance, the Master Choreographer and Chief Builder. Therefore let us adhere to the order of His blueprints, for we are "...*looking for the city which has foundations, whose architect and builder is God*" (Heb. 11:10 NASB).

PERSONAL DANCE STUDY JOURNAL

Principles and Practice

Principles and Practice

This Personal Dance Study Journal can be used by pastors, church leaders, or dance ministry leaders who are beginning new dance ministries within their local churches. It also is useful for participating dancers within an existing dance ministry. The questions can be adapted for each.

PRINCIPLE: Quotes from the chapter that have important principles to meditate on or consider within your context. Filling in the blank spaces with words found in the corresponding chapter helps the reader focus on key words within the principle.

PRACTICE: Focuses on applying the principle to your personal life or the lives of those around you, whether within the dance or worship ministries or the congregation as a whole. The questions are designed to go beyond the written text within the book and allow the Holy Spirit to speak to your heart.

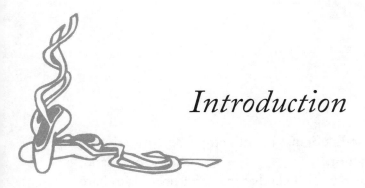

Introduction

PRINCIPLE

"With the world as our standard, we've most often witnessed a _____, _____ version of what
God originally created for a _____ and
_____ purpose."

PRACTICE

How has satan successfully convinced many Christians that dance is
carnal in nature? What examples of worldly dance have you witnessed or
participated in? How have these examples not fulfilled a pure or holy
purpose? Have you witnessed or personally experienced dance as a
powerful tool of ministry in worship, warfare, or celebration? How does
Acts 3:20-21 assure us that God will restore the dance?

_____

_____

_____

_____

_____

_____

_____

_____

PRINCIPLE

"It is time for God's original intent and purpose for creating dance to be taught in _____ ...On the one hand, there are those who...conclude that the safest policy is to have

_____ ...On the other hand, there are those who are experiencing an '_____ _____,' _____...without any sound teaching according to God's Word."

―――――――――――――⁓―――――――――――――

PRACTICE

Which of these extremes have you witnessed or personally experienced? What are the negative results in each of these imbalances?

_____

_____

_____

_____

_____

_____

_____

_____

_____

PRINCIPLE

"...before one considers the dance, he or she must have a
_____ _____ of and a _____ with
Jesus Christ...Unless there has been an _____
_____ of the spirit, dance used in the capacity of
praise and worship is nothing more than _____
_____ to Christian music. God is far more concerned with the _____ of your spirit than the
physical recreation of your body."

PRACTICE

Why is it necessary to have a personal relationship with God before you can worship Him in the dance? Is it possible to worship a
God you do not know or love? How can you become a dance ministry
that focuses on the spiritual and not only the physical?

_____

_____

_____

_____

_____

_____

_____

_____

_____

PRINCIPLE

"God seeks not the restoration of _____ but the
dance of the _____."

PRACTICE

What does this statement mean to you? How does a dancer's personal relationship with God affect the flow of the Holy Spirit through the dancer's ministry? Do you think movement in dance is spiritually effective if there is no real relationship with God? Does this mean all dancers within your ministry should have a fresh testimony of God's restoration in their lives?

_____

_____

_____

_____

_____

_____

_____

_____

_____

_____

_____

PRINCIPLE

"God deposited an understanding deep into my spirit that He had _____ me for and was _____ me to a ministry in dance."

PRACTICE

Do you have this same understanding about beginning a dance ministry in your church? Why is this important? Do you believe that some are attempting to be involved in dance ministry for the wrong reasons? What might some of these wrong reasons be? What are the dangers of this?

_____

_____

_____

_____

_____

_____

_____

_____

_____

_____

PRINCIPLE

"I share this….not as a dancer or a dance teacher, but a _____. Without _____, dance means nothing whatsoever to me."

PRACTICE

How can you establish your dances as worshipers first, and dancers second? Why is this so important?

_____

_____

_____

Dance

CHAPTER 1

The Dance on Trial

PRINCIPLE

"The subject now in question is that of the _____ and _____ of *dance in the church,*…God's _____ _____ for creating the dance unfortunately seemed lost."

PRACTICE

What validates dance in a church setting? Does the validity of dance depend on our opinion of it? What do you feel is the function of dance in the Church?

How has the world's use of dance adversely affected God's original plan for dance in the Church? Have you ever personally struggled with the idea of dance in worship due to the world's misuse of it?

_____

_____

_____

_____

_____

_____

_____

_____

PRINCIPLE

"Although it may seem that the enemy's trick had _____
_____ the Church, God always has a _____
that infinitely _____ and _____ that of the
enemy."

~

PRACTICE

Do you believe God has a strategy to restore dance to the Church?
Do you have any ideas as to what the steps of that strategy might en-
tail? Dancers can either 1) help execute God's plan or 2) through a
lack of knowledge bring additional damage to what has already been
done. How might this happen?

_____

_____

_____

_____

_____

_____

_____

PRINCIPLE

"Not only is there a _____ _____ to be waged
in repossessing what _____ belongs to us, but we

have perhaps an even greater war to be waged within
_____ _____ _____ to bring
_____, _____, and _____ to this
controversial area in the Church."

PRACTICE

Why is it important that there be biblical understanding concerning dance not only for the dancers but for the entire church? How will a biblical foundation help bring unity, understanding, and balance? How important is this revelation? How important is it to have the support of your pastor? How can you help your pastor better understand if he or she is still uncertain about the dance?

_____

_____

_____

_____

_____

_____

_____

_____

PRINCIPLE

"...Restoration of dance takes place when it is actively demonstrated in the natural by those who will _____, _____, and _____ respond to the _____ of the Holy Spirit, _____ to release through outward expression the _____ _____ of their hearts. When this is done in spirit and truth, it is beautifully saturated with the

evidence of God's presence. It instantly _____ and
_____ all previous charges or accusations against
the _____ and _____ of dance."

PRACTICE

What does this principle tell us are keys to having the presence of
God in our dance? Have you ever found it challenging to release your
innermost personal feelings and emotions through dance in the public setting of church? Has your ministry come under criticism and
judgment from fellow worshipers? What does your attitude need to
be? What would happen to the restoration of dance if all dancers quit
at the first criticism they received? In ministering to God's people
where is your primary focus, on the people or on God? What will it
take to dispel and disprove all previous accusations and mind-sets
against dance in the Church?

CHAPTER 2

Renewing Your Mind

PRINCIPLE

Romans 12:2, *and be not _____ to this world: but be ye _____ by the _____ of your mind, that ye may prove what is that _____, and _____, and _____, will of God.* "In rejecting the dance because of the _____ view that the world has presented, we are actually _____ to the world."

PRACTICE

How has the Church actually conformed to the world when it comes to many of the perceptions and decisions we have traditionally made concerning dance? Have our man-made traditions overpowered the truth of God's Word concerning dance?

_____

_____

_____

PRINCIPLE

Ecclesiastes 3:1-4, *To every thing there is a*_____, *and a time to* _____ _____ *under the heaven…a time to break down, and a time to* _____ _____…*a time to mourn, and a time to* _____.
"God's original purpose for dance has been _____ _____ but it is _____ the season and the time for its _____ to be revealed and rebuilt."

PRACTICE

Would God's Word say there is "a time to dance" if He were opposed to dance? What damage can be done by attempting to rebuild the dance on our own understanding of what we think seems right? What does Scripture say about what "seems right" to a man? (See Proverbs 16:25.) Are zeal, passion, and good intentions enough to build and restore the dance? Why not? If Scripture tells us there is a time to dance then there is also a time not to dance. Are you sensitive enough to the leading of the Spirit to discern the difference? Why is this discernment so important?

_____

_____

PRINCIPLE

"In Acts 10:9-16, Peter was praying when a vision came to him…The Lord spoke…What God has _____ and pronounced _____, do not _____ and _____ by regarding and calling common and _____ or _____."

―――――――――――⁓―――――――――――

PRACTICE

Peter had a difficult time accepting an understanding that differed from what he had settled in his mind to be true. How difficult might it be for people (even pastors) to accept dance when they have had a mind-set that it was wrong for the Church? Are you ready and willing to pay the price of being patient with those who still have a negative mind-set? Was Peter misunderstood by the other apostles? Did he allow their opinions to stop what he knew God had called him to do?

_____

_____

_____

_____

_____

_____

_____

_____

_____

_____

PRINCIPLE

"A _____worshiper will _____ the truth of God's Word over man's _____ in _____ area. God's Word is the _____ and _____ authority."

PRACTICE

Do you know scriptural truth about dance well enough that you could explain it to someone else? Suggestion: Make a personal study by writing down in a notebook your favorite Scriptures that support the dance.

_____

_____

_____

_____

PRINCIPLE

"What then is God's _____ _____ regarding the dance? It declares, *'Let them praise His name in the* _____' (Ps. 149:3a)."

PRACTICE

Does this command speak to all believers or just trained dancers? Who are the "them" that the command is directed toward?

_____

_____

_____

_____

_____

CHAPTER 3

Original Purpose

PRINCIPLE

Romans 11:36a (AMP), *For* _____ *Him and*
_____ *Him and* _____ *Him are all*
things. [For _____ _____ *things* _____
with Him and _____ _____ *Him…* "Satan
is no _____; he is only out to _____ and
_____ God's creation."

PRACTICE

How do we know that satan could not have created dance? Can
you fully explain this concept to someone who does not understand it?
What would you say?

_____

_____

_____

_____

_____

_____

PRINCIPLE

Revelation 4:11, *Thou are worthy, O Lord to receive* _____ *and* _____ *and* _____ *: for Thou has created* _____ _____ *, and for Thy* _____ *they are and were* _____ *. Psalm 149:3a, Let them* _____ *His name in the* _____ *. Psalm 149:4a, For the Lord taketh* _____ *in His people.* "This word, *pleasure*, is a Hebrew word, which means 'to be _____ with, to _____, be _____,'…God not only favorably _____ and _____ of dance, He also sets His _____ on it, finding _____, _____, and _____ in it."

<hr>

PRACTICE

How can this sequence of Scriptures be useful in you helping others to biblically see God's purpose and approval for the dance? How important is it for dancers to know these basic Scriptures and be able to quote them? Psalm 149:3 says to praise Him in the dance. What does verse four say about how God feels about it? When the Scripture says, "let them" is this only a suggestion or is it a command? How can this be a sound argument in favor of dance to churches that will not allow dance since the Word clearly says to "let them" not to "stop them."

_____

_____

_____

_____

_____

_____

_____

_____

PRINCIPLE

"Not only have I witnessed the demonstration of the _____ _____ bringing _____ to those who had not previously known Christ, but I have also seen how it ____ _____ a new _____ and _____ into the afflicted, _____ them from _____ _____ that possess them and hold them captive."

~~~~~

PRACTICE

Have you witnessed either of these things? How can dance be instrumental in someone receiving salvation? How can dance be used to release those who are oppressed? Can the power of ministering the Word through dance be equally as powerful as ministering it through preaching? How is a dance minister a dancing preacher? Do you believe a picture is worth 1000 words? How can the visual aspect of dance add power to the ministry of the audible word?

_____

_____

_____

_____

_____

_____

_____

_____

_____

_____

_____

_____

_____

PRINCIPLE

"Dance was created to be a _____, _____ tool of communication in the Kingdom of God to His glory. Dance is a _____-_____ _____ in the hands of the believer as it _____ and _____ God's Word; and it _____ the _____ of that Word to bring _____ to the afflicted and _____ to those who were bound."

PRACTICE

The principle above explains why satan has tried so hard to distort and destroy the dance from operating as a two-edged sword in our hands. What is a two-edged sword a type of? If dance conveys the power of the Word, how important is it for the dancer to have a personal revelation of the words they are dancing to?

_____

_____

_____

_____

_____

_____

_____

_____

PRINCIPLE

"The very last biblical account that uses the word dance is in reference to the _____ of the _____ _____. The _____ of his repentance and reunion with the father was _____ expressed by _____, _____, and _____ in the father's house. Therefore, we see dance is strongly connected with _____, _____, _____, _____, and _____."

PRACTICE

According to the New Testament story of the prodigal son found in Luke 15, repentance and reunion with the father were appropriately expressed by music and dancing in the father's house. How can this be a sound argument to those who think dance was only for Old Testament times? How can we relate this to the validity of dance in the Church? Is the Church the Father's house? Did Jesus himself say there was dancing in the Father's house? Could this be another sound biblical argument for you to add to your notebook of favorite Scriptures that prove dance belongs in the (church) Father's house?

_____
_____
_____
_____
_____
_____

PRINCIPLE

Jeremiah 30:19b (NASB), *And from them shall proceed _____ and the voice of those who make _____ _____[____].... Jeremiah 31:13 (NASB), Then the virgin shall _____ in the _____, and the young men and the old, together, for I will turn their _____ into _____, and will _____ them, and give them _____ for their sorrow.*

PRACTICE

Look at the context of the verses above: Jeremiah 30:3,8,16-19 (NASB) and Jeremiah 31:4,11-13 (NASB). What groups of people do these verses tell us will be part of the dance? Does it surprise you who is included? Why is dance not just reserved for pretty little maidens?

_____
_____
_____
_____
_____
_____

CHAPTER 4

The Roots of Corruption

PRINCIPLE

"Dance was created for _____. It is a _____ part of God's plan for worship...Worship gives great _____, _____, and _____ to God. It functions as the most _____, _____, _____ form of communion between _____ and _____."

PRACTICE

How does expression through dance help you to feel a more intimate connection with God and why? Would you feel less of a personal connection if you were no longer allowed to move or express your worship through any kind of outward expression? Is it possible to express any emotion without using your physical body in any way?

_____

_____

_____

_____

_____

_____

_____

_____

_____

PRINCIPLE

"Lucifer's name literally meant "to _____."......When Lucifer was cast out of the heavens, he received a _____ _____ from God. ...God now addressed him as _____, meaning _____, _____, _____, the _____, the _____, and he was cast out. ...pride and jealousy led him to betray God....satan coveted God's _____. However, God will not give His _____ to another; He _____ it as His own _____."

PRACTICE

What significance do you think the name change was to the devil? When you dance, does it draw man's attention to God or to yourself? Have you ever wanted to be noticed, complemented, or praised for your worship dancing? How can this be the same sin lucifer fell into? How does our pride and jealousy change our worship, and how could it harm our dance ministry? How can we avoid pride and jealousy within our own worship team? How can we promote unity and love between the dancers? Why is this unity a vital necessity?

_____

_____

_____

_____

_____

_____

_____

_____

_____

_____

_____

_____

_____

_____

PRINCIPLE

"The product he (lucifer) promoted was _____. And what gave his sales technique such power? It was his God-given _____ to glorify through his _____, _____, _____, and his _____ to excel in these areas."

PRACTICE

Since we have been created for God's glory and given a wide variety of gifts and talents with which to worship God, is it possible for us to also merchandise God's glory? Has your ministry become more focused on picking the right music, designing garments, practicing choreography etc. than it has been with the focus and purpose of God Himself? How would this be easy to fall into? How can we bring checks and balances to our ministry so this does not happen to us?

_____

_____

_____

Dance

CHAPTER 5

Dance in the World

PRINCIPLE

"Worldly dance does not reflect God's _____, and it is a _____ of God's original _____ for creating it…Dance was created as an _____, _____ _____ of communication and its _____ or _____ value depends upon how it is _____."

PRACTICE

Is dance moral, immoral, or amoral? What does amoral mean? Can dance be used for either good or evil? How would you explain to someone the difference between worldly dance and Christian dance? Carefully choose words that non-Christians would understand. How can your explanation be a tool of evangelism? Give an example of how worldly dance reflects, promotes, and encourages the kingdom of this world and its ways? Should Christians dance to worldly music?

PRINCIPLE

"Dancers beware, for dance was created with the
_____ to _____ the _____
of man. Emotions are a powerful part of _____
_____, and the _____ to a man's soul is a
_____ one to open if the _____ you bring
is not one of _____. Dance is a _____ and
_____ gift, full of untapped _____ _____...it is a
beautiful art form that can _____ the _____,
_____, and _____, either for _____ or
_____."

PRACTICE

Explain how the dance of Herodias' daughter excited Herod's emotions and caused the death of John the Baptist. How can we prevent our dance moves and even our dance garments from causing the emotions of a man's soul to be drawn away from God? How can our garments and choreography either support or damage the purpose God?

_____
_____
_____
_____
_____
_____
_____
_____
_____

PRINCIPLE

"One of the reasons that dance affects the _____ of man
so _____ is due to the fact that it is an _____.
Dance is part of the _____ _____ of man."

PRACTICE

Explain how dance is an instinct. How have you seen this to be
true in your experience? If we are created in God's image, does God
dance? Explain this in light of Zephaniah 3:17.

_____
_____
_____
_____
_____
_____
_____
_____

PRINCIPLE

"Remembering that the dance will either _____ or _____, consider this: In Zephaniah 3:18…*God says, 'I will* _____ *them that are sorrowful for the* _____ _____.' This passage is an exciting revelation for the _____ of dance; it clearly reflects the God-given _____ and _____ of the dance to _____, or _____ unto the Lord."

PRACTICE

Explain how dance can function as something that scatters or something that gathers. How can we conduct our ministry so that we continuously gather? Do you see the serious responsibility that dancers carry before the Lord because they could powerfully affect others for either good or evil? Have you ever seen a dance in church that would cause onlookers to be more apt to scatter from Christ than to gather toward Him? Give an example. Have you ever witnessed a dance that clearly caused onlookers to gather toward Christ? Give an example.

_____

_____

_____

_____

_____

_____

_____

_____

PRINCIPLE

"…worldly dance is an _____ to the dancer, for it becomes the _____ of _____ and _____

_____ as one seeks to move up the ladder...God created dance for _____, not to be _____...Another aspect of worldly dance is that of _____ _____...This keeps the focus of the dancer on _____ and _____ more of it."

PRACTICE

Were you drawn to a ministry in dance because of your love for dance or your love for God? What constitutes an idol and how is it possible to make even worship dance an idol? What spiritual safeguards should we make for our worship dancers to avoid idolatry and selfish ambition? Give an example of what could be idolatry in dance. Give an example of what could be selfish ambition in dance. How is the focus of worship dancers completely different than the focus of worldly dancers? Who and what is Christian dance all about? Who and what is worldly dance is all about? Will the power of God flow through a dance team if there is competition and jealousy among the members?

Dance

CHAPTER 6

Glorify God in Your Body

PRINCIPLE

"Somewhere along the line, the _____ that the believer's physical body is _____ in nature has crept into the Church. Unfortunately, the _____ of the Church at large has _____ under this deception...He (god) has honored these _____ vessels with the deposit of the _____ _____. They are _____ to Him, and He asks that we _____ them back to Him for His _____."

PRACTICE

Read Romans 12:1 in several translations and write the verse in your own words. How does this verse apply to the ministry of dance?

_____

_____

_____

_____

_____

_____

_____

_____

PRINCIPLE

"Every movement that we choose to make throughout the day is a level of _____, _____ service— whether we are cleaning toilets or lying prostrate before the Lord. Each action may, however, express a different _____ or _____ of _____."

PRACTICE

On a large scale can you see how faithfulness in your daily movements may express a level of worship before God? What daily, practical, service-oriented movements can you think of that could be considered worshipful service before the Lord? For example: Are you a good Christian husband, wife, son, daughter, employee, homemaker, student etc.? How do these daily worshipful expressions effect your ministry in the dance?

_____

_____

_____

_____

_____

_____

_____

_____

_____

_____

_____

_____

PRINCIPLE

"The word *consummate* is defined as _____ _____.
…True consummation, complete fulfillment, in your worship is not found in _____ a _____ or _____ a
_____ such as _____, _____ your _____,
or _____. True fulfillment _____ _____
with a _____ of _____ and the _____ of
_____ that is within you, which creates a _____,
or _____, of _____ between man and God."

PRACTICE

Have you ever experienced this level of fulfillment in your personal
worship? How can worship expressions become lifeless or meaning-
less if your heart is not humble or truthful before God? How can
being still before God also be very powerful in times of worship? Why
do you think it is an important balance for dancers to know how and
when to be still and quiet as well as to know when it is time to dance?

_____

_____

_____

_____

_____

_____

_____

_____

_____

_____

_____

_____

PRINCIPLE

"The Greek and Hebrew definitions of the words used for *praise* and *worship* are clearly defined by _____ _____ and _____ such as _____, _____, _____, _____, _____ of _____, _____, _____, _____, even _____ _____. These expressions are _____ reactions to _____ emotions. This is how we _____ _____ God."

PRACTICE

When you experience different emotions, is it natural to have a physical response? How have you expressed the emotion of joy? Sadness? Reverence? How can these emotions be expressed through the ministry of dance? Is suppressing your emotions or hiding behind false emotions a common event in the church setting? Could your honest expression of emotion be used by God to set free others who may be afraid to allow themselves to express what they are feeling?

_____

_____

_____

_____

_____

_____

_____

_____

_____

_____

_____

_____

_____

_____

_____

_____

PRINCIPLE

"The single best overall definition I have found for the word *rejoice* is, 'the act of _____ _____.' It seems it would be impossible to _____ without any type of _____ or _____...But the traditions of man have told God's children that it is not _____ _____ for them to rejoice in their _____ for their Father and to _____ in _____ it...It only stands to reason, if we are to _____ God in our bodies, then we must _____ and _____ them in some fashion."

PRACTICE

Have you allowed yourself to go to the next level of expressing the praise and worship you feel in your heart for God? Have you ever personally, without being told, lifted your hands, bowed, knelt down, shouted, or moved your feet in an act of declaration, honor, or celebration of your love for God? Do some dancers find it hard to express themselves if there is no choreography? Why is it important for dancers to be able to express themselves spontaneously in dance as well as through choreographed dance? How can you help develop this freedom in your worship dance team?

_____

_____

_____

_____

_____

_____

_____

_____

_____

_____

PRINCIPLE

Second Samuel 6:14-16, *And David _____ before the Lord with _____ _____ _____ ...And...Michal Saul's daughter [David's wife] looked through a window, and saw David _____ and _____ before the Lord; and she _____ him in her _____. "...Michal did not join Israel's _____ of the return of the ark of _____ _____. She _____ _____ _____ and watched through her*

window. This is exactly where satan wants to keep God's people—in the position of a _____ _____, believing
that is the _____ _____ to be."

PRACTICE:

Michal would not dance. What parallels do you see between Michal
and the Church as it has despised and judged open expressions of
worship like dance? Have you found yourself judging another's
expression of worship as Michal did David's? How can dancing out
spontaneously in the church setting be an act of humility? How could it
also become a prideful act? Are dancers always at risk of being
wrongfully judged? Are you willing to pay that price? How can this
become a spiritual battle in the mind of the dancer? What price did
Michal pay for judging King David's dance? What is the definition of
the word *barren*? What is this a spiritual type of?

_____

_____

_____

_____

_____

_____

_____

_____

_____

_____

_____

_____

_____

Dance

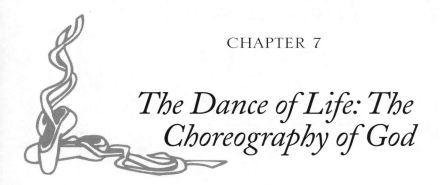

CHAPTER 7

The Dance of Life: The Choreography of God

PRINCIPLE

"On a very large scale, all the planets of the universe _____ and _____ in a _____ of perfect _____ and _____ according to the _____ _____ and _____ _____ of God, the _____ _____ of life. On a much smaller scale, the very makeup and fabric of the human body also _____ in a _____ and _____ _____ dance of life. ...The rhythm of our heart beats faithfully day and night without any voluntary assistance on our part. Involuntarily, our lungs expand and contract, breathing the breath of life.

PRACTICE

God displays His splendor as the Master Choreographer in the dance of life as all creation, large and small, move in a cosmic dance of perfectly designed timing and order. There is however another dimension to the dance of life whose steps move to the tune of the free will of man. How are the steps we choose in life like a dance before God?

_____

_____

_____

_____

_____

_____

_____

_____

PRINCIPLE

"The truth is that the _____ of our dance of life are _____ in _____ with, and in _____ to, the honoring of either _____, _____, or _____. This is all _____ by our _____ _____, for we have been given by God the _____ to _____ and _____ the _____ of our life."

PRACTICE

As much as God take 1s pleasure in a "dance of life" that would honor Him, He does not move us through the steps of our life like puppets on a string. How does "free will" make our choice to worship God in dance so special? How does our "dance of life" prove and reveal the true heart within us? Can God worship Himself in the dance or is this a special gift we can give Him that He can not give Himself? According to Isaiah 43:6-7, what were we created for? How does dance glorify God? What is the definition of the word *choreography*?

_____

_____

_____

_____

_____

_____

_____

_____

_____

PRINCIPLE

"Some people feel that if a dance is not created as a
_____, spur-of-the-moment expression, it is no
_____ of the _____ ...Just because something is _____ and _____ in advance does not
_____ it from being _____ _____ from
the _____ of God."

PRACTICE

Have you experienced the controversy concerning choreographed dance in the church? How do you answer this accusation? How is this accusation a deception of a foundational truth concerning anything written down for us to learn?

_____

_____

_____

_____

_____

_____

_____

_____

PRINCIPLE

"The calling of the choreographer in the house of the Lord is a _____ _____ that should be _____ _____ and _____ as God has given these persons the ability to clearly _____ and _____ _____ His _____ in the demonstration of _____ and _____."

PRACTICE

What is a "calling"? Why does a choreographer in a dance ministry need to have such a calling? How is it prophetic? Why is this so important? What does this tell us about who we should let choreograph our dances in our ministries? Would it be better to have no dance at all than to create a dance that was not inspired or directed from God? Why? In the Old Testament, how many years of apprenticeship did the temple dancers have to submit to in order to be allowed to participate as members of the regular chorus? How does this speak of the importance of patience and proper preparation for dance ministry in the house of God?

_____

_____

_____

_____

_____

_____

_____

_____

_____

_____

_____

_____

_____

_____

PRINCIPLE

"In mastering any skill, it is God's desire that we _____ and _____ that talent, developing it to its _____ _____ to the _____, _____, and _____ of God...It would be hard to develop a gift to the point of being addressed as _____ if you never _____. Becoming skillful is _____ to _____; yet choreographed dance has been _____ for this very characteristic."

PRACTICE

Why is training important in any area of our ministry? How can the time and dedication we devote in developing our skill and knowledge for the glory of God be seen as an act of devotion, self-sacrifice, and worship? How is this compared to walking worthy of your calling? What does Ephesians 4:1 say about walking worthy of our calling? Who was Chenaniah? Why was he chosen to lead? What does his name mean? What does it mean to be "planted of the Lord" in your ministry? Why would the choreographer need to be well studied in the Word of God?

_____

_____

Dance

CHAPTER 8

Extreme Worship and Spiritual Freedom

PRINCIPLE

"The word *extreme* when used in context with the word *worship* may automatically trigger a _____ _____ by those who might _____ picture and _____ _____ _____, wildly _____ worship service. In reality, the word *extreme* is a _____, _____, _____ description of an _____, or _____, of worship that encompasses _____ that is within us. The word *extreme* is defined as meaning "_____, in the _____ _____, _____, far from what is _____ or _____, very _____, _____."

PRACTICE

Negative interpretations of the word *extreme* can be *too much, going too far, or going beyond what is acceptable.* Do you believe that expressive forms of worship such as dance can easily be seen this way by traditional viewpoints? Does the word *extreme* trigger in you a negative or positive response when used to describe worship? What does extreme worship mean to you in the positive sense? In your experience, have you ever feared out-of-control worship services? Whose control do we fear being out of: man's or God's? Can being in the flesh be considered being out of God's control? Why is it necessary for those who are restoring the dance to have spiritual discernment? Can you see how the dance cannot be restored without encountering many road blocks along the way? What difficulties have you encountered?

PRINCIPLE

"It is sad but true that many of us, from our earliest days, have spent more time learning _____ _____ to _____ than _____ _____ _____. Responding to God is the _____ of _____ worship, and God _____ for us to _____ and _____ _____ to Him."

PRACTICE

What do you think the difference is between worshiping in an outward, biblical form versus worshiping in a way that "seems" safe and acceptable? Have you personally been effected by the tradition that taught you it was inappropriate to openly respond to God in church? Why is it difficult for this mind-set to be overcome? Would you rather play it safe or risk reaching out beyond your comfort zone to touch the heart of God? Why does the enemy fear extreme worship?

_____

_____

_____

_____

_____

_____

_____

_____

_____

_____

PRINCIPLE

John 4:23-24, *But the hour cometh, and now is, when the _____ worshippers shall worship the Father in _____ and in _____: for the Father _____ such to worship Him. God is a Spirit: and they that worship Him ____ worship Him in _____ and in _____.* "*Must* is a very strong word; therefore, in seeking worship of the _____ _____, _____, and _____, it is important for us to begin to understand what God means by _____ and _____."

PRACTICE

If God not only seeks but requires that we " must " worship Him in spirit and truth , what do the terms "spirit" and "truth" mean to you concerning worship? Is it possible to perform a so-called Christian dance and not be worshiping in either spirit or truth? Do you think God receives or is pleased with a worship dance when the dancer's personal life is the opposite of the words the dancer is attempting to portray? How is this untruthful?

_____

_____

_____

_____

_____

_____

_____

_____

_____

_____

_____

PRINCIPLE

Second Corinthians 3:17b, *Where the Spirit of the Lord is, there is* _____. "This word, liberty, in the Greek means freedom...Our freedom is a _____, _____ and _____ matter, and it is by no means _____. Freedom is something that must be _____ for...there is no true freedom in _____ for man without this spiritual _____ that has been _____ for us by Christ."

PRACTICE

How was your spiritual freedom purchased? What price was paid so that you might dance in God's house? How will remembering the high cost of your freedom keep you humble as you minister? Is it possible to worship in spirit and truth without freedom? How can a lack of freedom hinder our worship? How does the enemy constantly work to steal our spiritual freedom? How can the simplicity of a single tear or a lifted hand be extreme worship?

_____

_____

_____

_____

_____

_____

_____

_____

_____

_____

PRINCIPLE

John 8:32, *And ye shall know the* _____, *and the* _____ *shall make you* _____. "This simply means that what we are ____ in our worship through song or movement must be the _____. ...Movement in worship is not for the sake of _____. It must be a _____, _____ expression of the _____ ...Worshiping in truth eliminates all ____ _____ _____ that is acted out simply because someone _____ it to you as the _____ thing to do at a _____ time."

PRACTICE

Although we see dance as a fresh expression of worship in contemporary church settings, we must realize that it can also become just another ritualistic traditional expression. Give an example of how a worship expression such as lifting your hands might fall into this ritualistic, robotic response and become void of life. Do you lift your hands out of an overflowing expression? Can you see how the dance cannot be restored without encountering many road blocks and bumps in the road? What was God's "due order" a type of? Describe the lesson of complete abandon that was learned from the choir of birds singing. How is this extreme worship?

CHAPTER 9

Dance and the Anointing

PRINCIPLE

"Any attempt to execute the dance as a _____ without the _____ is nothing more than _____ to Christian music. We must reiterate that the dance in itself is _____—neither good nor evil. It is not the dance itself that has the _____ to break _____ _____ but the _____ of God as it works through the _____ as a _____ and _____ of that _____."

PRACTICE

Explain how the function of the anointing through dance ministry is much like that of a telephone wire. How did the missing piece of Abigail's puzzle leave her and her mother feeling and why? How can we relate this to the missing element of dance in worship?

_____

_____

_____

_____

_____

_____

_____

_____

_____

PRINCIPLE

"Not only does dance belong as a _____, _____ part of God's picture, but, equally as important, it needs to be _____ _____ and ___ _____ with the other parts of the picture as God _____ _____ and _____ it to be….(there are) four things that can happen to affect the _____ of the _____ of dance in relation to the Body of Christ. It can be 1)_____ , 2)_____ (Stage I), 3)_____ (Stage II), or 4)_____ (properly) _____."

PRACTICE

List two reasons why the puzzle piece that was lost under the deck was a type of worldly dance. How can the dance team work in unity with the worship team? Is it important for the worship team to understand the scriptural function of the dance? Perhaps you could share your favorite Scriptures on dance with the worship leader to help bring unity.

_____

_____

_____

_____
_____
_____
_____
_____
_____
_____

PRINCIPLE

...As we choose Christ, we not only _____ unto _____, but we, in turn, _____ unto _____ in the Kingdom of God. The _____, _____ dancer does not and cannot minister_____."

PRACTICE

Disconnected:

Why is it impossible for an un-saved worldly dance to minister Christ and His anointing? If a body part such as your arm were completely cut off, would it continue to live and function in its created purpose? How can this parallel the worldly dancer who does not know Christ or His purpose for creating dance?

_____
_____
_____
_____
_____
_____
_____

PRINCIPLE

"Being dislocated is definitely a step _____ from being disconnected, for now you are a _____, _____ member of the Body of Christ. Even so, this state does not _____ the _____ of God's overall plan. For it is possible to have living, connected body parts and still be dysfunctional due to an improper or faulty connection." Ephesians 2:10, *For we are His _____, created in Christ Jesus unto _____ _____, which God hath _____ _____ that we should _____ in them.*

PRACTICE

Dislocated Stage 1:

Describe the difference between being disconnected from the Body of Christ and being dislocated in the Body of Christ. How is dislocation a step up from being disconnected? If a Christian is struggling to function in a ministry they are not called to, what is this a type of? If you succeed in forcing your puzzle piece into the wrong location what will the results be? How does this affect the other Body members? Do you believe there are those attempting to be dancers who are not called? How does this harm the restoration of dance? What does the word *ordained* mean in Ephesians 2:10? Do you feel *ordained* to the dance ministry in your church? In light of Ephesians 2:10 are we allowed to choose our calling?

_____

_____

_____

_____

_____

PRINCIPLE

"*Dislocation*" most commonly means _____ _____
_____, or not _____ _____. Being _____
and _____ are two very important factors, but you
must also allow God to _____ you. Dance is a ministry that goes far beyond having the _____ to dance. It
is a _____ that requires you to _____ God with
all your _____, _____, _____, and _____. It
also requires _____ and _____ _____ to the
_____ of the Spirit. These things come only through
a _____ _____ with God...."

PRACTICE

Dislocated Stage 2:

Is it possible to be operating in your ordained calling yet still be
"out of joint?" Explain why. Even if you are a Christian and also a
skillful, gifted dancer does this automatically make you a dance minister? Why not? Have you ever found the right location for the right
puzzle piece only to struggle in an attempt to force it into its place in
the wrong way? What is this a type of? Can this happen in the dance
ministry? Is having a love and zeal for God enough to accomplish the
anointing in your ministry? What else is necessary?

_____

_____

_____

_____

_____

_____

_____

_____

PRINCIPLE

"…many spiritual areas of our lives must be _____ _____ and _____ _____ according to the _____ and _____ of God's holy _____ before _____, _____ ministry can take place…God's Word is our _____, bringing _____ between the _____ and the _____. …As ministers in the Body of Christ, we are called to be _____ and _____. We must be in proper _____ with the Head so that we may, in turn, _____ the _____ to flow from the Head as an oil to the _____."

PRACTICE

Properly Connected:

As Christians, whose Body are we members of? Read Psalm 133:1-2. Who is the head or high priest a type of? What is the definition of the name "Christ"? Why is it necessary that Christians in the Body be properly connected to the Head if we want the anointing in our dance? Biblically, what is the precious oil a type of? What is the beard of the high priest a type of? Will the anointing flow through immaturity? How can dance be considered priesthood? Read Exodus 30:32. What is the flesh spiritually a type of and why is the anointing not to be poured upon it? Is it possible to be in the flesh and have the anointing in your dance? Why did God tell them not to copy the anointing? Can the true anointing be copied or counterfeited? Why not?

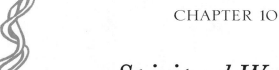

CHAPTER 10

Spiritual Warfare and the Dance

PRINCIPLE

"Although praise and worship are powerful _____ of
_____, applying them does not create a _____
_____. One cannot simply say, "_____ _____
_____," and have all his or her troubles _____.
There was always great _____, _____, and _____,
along with the true heartfelt _____ and _____,
that caused the praises of God's people to be _____
_____ against their enemies."

PRACTICE

Why would the enemy want to remove this chapter from the book?
Does your dance ministry take the time to teach and practice the
principles of prayer, faith, and humility? Are these principles optional
if we are to demonstrate spiritual power to set the captives free and
defeat the enemy?

_____

_____

_____

_____

_____

_____

_____

_____

PRINCIPLE

Prayer, faith, humility, praise and worship combine in the story of King Jehoshaphat in Second Chronicles chapter 20. "…they now advanced with nothing more than _____ in their _____ and the _____ of God on their _____. …Not only did this faithful demonstration of praise _____ the people from the enemy, but it also _____ the enemy."

PRACTICE

Read Psalm 149 (which specifically mentions praise dancers). How does this praise effect the enemy compared to the praises of Jehosaphat's army? Do you see why the enemy does not want us to understand the spiritual power of the dance? Read Second Chronicles chapter 20 to refresh yourself with the context of this principle. Then outline for yourself the references to prayer, humility, faith, and praise and worship that are contained in the passage. Do these principles make sense in the natural? Is this why it is called "spiritual" warfare?

_____

_____

_____

_____

_____

_____

_____

_____

_____

_____

_____

_____

PRINCIPLE

"We also must not overlook the _____ that praise
has to _____ not only those who are _____, but also
those who are _____...Such worship is _____
_____ against those things that hold us _____, not
only for the _____, but for the _____ as well."

PRACTICE

Read Acts 16:25-26. How did the atmosphere of praise and worship change the physical conditions of every prison where Paul and Silas were held? Were there other blessings other than the physical that were manifested that night? How important is it for those participating in our dance ministries to choose to praise rather than complain when they face the many battles that arise in the restoration of dance? Why does a dance minister need to be strong in spiritual battle?

_____

_____

_____

_____

_____

_____

_____

PRINCIPLE

"Ushering in the presence of God through our _____ and _____ is like turning on a _____ in a dark room: There is no _____, for where there is _____, there is no _____. Scripture tells us 'submit you therefore to God. Resist the devil, and he will flee from you' (James 4:7). When we submit to God's direction in the _____ concerning the principles of _____ and _____, we are also ____ the devil and his _____ against us by using _____ that God specifically designed for our _____ and _____."

PRACTICE

By submitting to God's directions to praise Him in the dance we resist the devil, and he flees. Therefore it only makes sense that the devil would not want us to dance. Have you experienced the many different tactics the devil uses to try and hinder your dance? Share some of your experiences. How important is it for the dancer to recognize satan's tactics and step out faithfully in the dance, using it as a spiritual weapon of warfare?

_____

_____

_____

_____

_____

_____

_____

_____

_____

_____

_____

_____

_____

_____

PRINCIPLE

Some of the most _____ and _____ information concerning the dance and it's _____ for the Church in this area is to be found in _____ and _____. We have _____ foundational _____ blocks consisting of the following things: 1) _____ is to praise, 2) _____ to praise, 3) _____ to praise, and 4) _____ to praise.

1) Who

Building block number one is _____ and _____ —who is to praise God?

PRACTICE

Read through building block number one and to the best of your ability answer this question:

1) Who is to praise?

_____

_____

PRINCIPLE

2) Where?

Building block number two is short and_____. Is it to praise Him, or in this case, where is it scriptural to praise the Lord in the dance?

_____

_____

———————————⌢———————————

PRACTICE

Read through building block number two and answer the question: Where are we to praise the Lord? List two Scriptures that verify dancing in a church setting.

_____

_____

_____

_____

_____

_____

_____

_____

PRINCIPLE

3) How?

Building block number three, _____ to praise Him, breaks _____ into what I call the basic four _____ of worship, which are the following:

1) _____

2) _____

3) _____

4) _____

—⁓—

PRACTICE

List Scriptures that support each cornerstone.

1) The Word of God

_____

2) Singing

_____

3) Musical instruments

_____

4) Dance

_____

PRINCIPLE

4) The _____ building blocks of _____ and _____ can be broken down into _____ specific areas. Why do we praise the Lord? Consider the following four _____ taken from our _____ Psalms.

—⁓—

PRACTICE

Fill in the four reasons listed in the Psalms for why we praise the Lord.

1) _____

2) _____

3) _____

4) _____

CHAPTER 11

Beautiful Feet (Proclaiming the Good Tidings)

PRINCIPLE

Isaiah 52:7, *How* _____ *upon the mountains are the* _____ *of him that bringeth* _____ _____, *that* _____*; that bringeth good tidings of* _____, *that* _____ _____*; that saith unto Zion, Thy God* _____*!* "Our feet and their use as a spiritual type must not be _____ as we seek God's _____ in the restoration of dance. The Hebrew word we translate *publish* means to tell, declare, cause to, let or make to hear; proclaim, proclamation, report, or show forth.

———⁓———

PRACTICE

What does the Scripture say about our feet as we proclaim the gospel (good tidings)? The power to communicate through physical demonstrations of your body language can be as simple as basic moves such as walking, marching, skipping, or stomping. Can you see how extensive dance training is not the only way to use your feet to proclaim God?

What does Psalm 150:6 tell us about who can praise God in the dance? Why is the addition of bodily movement so powerful?

_____

_____

_____

_____

_____

_____

_____

PRINCIPLE

The word *celebrate*, as found in Nahum 1:15 (NASB), is the Hebrew word _____, meaning to _____ in a _____, to _____ in a _____ _____; to _____ a _____; to be _____; to _____; to _____; to keep or hold a _____ _____; to _____ to and fro…Dance was such an integral part of how the Israelites _____ the _____ that to _____ a feast literally refers to _____, _____ to and from, and _____ in the dance."

PRACTICE

What two words are both translated from the same Hebrew word, *chagag*? What does chagag mean? What does Psalms 68:11-12 say happens when the women proclaim the good tidings? How is this picture of the power of dance in spiritual warfare? These women were called a great host, what does that mean? In Psalm 68:24-25 we see a great procession into the sanctuary. What three groups of people were mentioned? Do you see the similarity to the basic four cornerstones of worship we studied in the previous chapter? Name the Scripture that tells us what has damaged or even eliminated these great processionals into the sanctuary?

_____

_____

_____

_____

_____

_____

_____

_____

PRINCIPLE

"The direct connection between _____ and the use of our _____ as a spiritual type is found throughout Scripture. Remember, it is the serpent as a type of satan who has been _____ by God with no _____ with which to walk upright…the Word of God provides us with this type of putting our _____ on the _____ of our _____."

PRACTICE

Look up the following Scriptures and summarize what you find about the power and significance of the use of our feet as a spiritual type:

Romans 16:19-20 (NASB) _____

Joshua 1:3 (NASB) _____

Joshua 3:15-16 (NASB) _____

Joshua 4:18 (NASB) _____

2 Samuel 22:38-39 (NASB) _____

Psalm 8:6 (KJV) _____

Psalm 47:1-3 (NASB) _____

Psalm 108:12-13 (KJV)_____

Luke 10:19 (KJV) _____

Joshua 10:24-25 (NASB) _____

Genesis 3:14 (KJV) _____

CHAPTER 12

Order in theRestoration

PRINCIPLE

"It is impossible for us to come into the _____ of what was originally _____ for the _____ if we do not _____ after God's _____ _____. Biblical order does not always include what _____ think seems _____, but it is _____ to God's _____ as He has _____ in His _____."

PRACTICE

Who were the characters in Leviticus 10:1-3 killed by God? What key line in this Scripture tells us why God was so displeased? Was their offering acknowledged as hallowed? Why not?

_____

_____

_____

_____

PRINCIPLE

"Praise God! He has _____ a _____ for us to _____
_____ Him, but we must realize that God's _____ has
not _____. ...I believed much of the worship existing in
the Church today is not _____ as _____, for it is not according to what _____ _____; it is more in line with
what seems _____ to a _____."

~~~

PRACTICE

What is the end result according to Proverbs 14:12 when we do
things man's way, even if it "seems" right to us? How can we parallel this
to Nadab and Abihu? Is obeying God's instructions to "let them" praise
His name with dancing an optional issue in church worship? Does "let
them" mean everyone has to dance or does it mean to let those who want
to? Should everyone have to play a musical instrument because God says
to praise Him with music? What do we desire most, keeping our comfortable traditions or pleasing God by obeying His Word? How does the
restoration of dance in worship show honor to God?

_____
_____
_____
_____
_____
_____
_____
_____

PRINCIPLE

I understand that the transition from _____ _____ to
the more _____, _____ _____ can be difficult and

uncomfortable at first…For the most part, this responsibility lies in the _____ of the _____. You might be surprised at how _____ the people will _____ to
new _____ of worship as they are introduced with
the _____ of _____ and a heart that clearly
_____ a _____ to _____ God."

PRACTICE

Consider the worship in your local church. Have there been any
transitions in the form of outward expressions? Are there transitions
that have yet to take place? How can these transitions be made with
the least resistance? What would be the best strategy to convince
those who doubt or fear the appropriateness of outward expression?
What does Scripture tell us about knowing the truth? How important
is biblical teaching in renewing our minds? What role does the leadership of the church play in establishing permission and freedom to
grow in biblical worship?

_____

_____

_____

_____

_____

_____

_____

_____

PRINCIPLE

"The order of the restoration of dance is much like that of
_____ a _____. …Building in order is _____

a _____ _____. ...many so-called dance ministries come quickly on the scene only to _____ and _____. Good intentions are _____ _____. Many have attempted to _____ God's _____ for dance only to sadly watch it perish in their church for _____ of _____."

PRACTICE

Why do so many dance ministries not survive? Look up Hosea 4:6 and Proverbs 19:2. What do they teach you about the importance of knowledge? Can we be priests for God without the knowledge of God? How is rushing compared to sin? Look up First Corinthians 3:11. What foundation needs to be laid before a dance ministry is started in a church?

_____

_____

_____

_____

_____

_____

_____

_____

_____

_____

_____

PRINCIPLE

"Being overly excited and emotional can be _____ if it causes you to move out _____ _____ _____. God will not allow His _____ to be treated with _____—whether _____ or _____."

<hr />

PRACTICE

Study this chapter concerning the story of David bringing up the ark. How does David's excitement in moving out in the flesh parallel that of many in the dance ministry today? What was God's "due order" and how can we see this as a warning to dance ministries? Discuss the spiritual types of 1)the ark, 2) the oxen/new cart, 3) Uzza touching the ark, 4) the threshing floor. How does each of these warn us against errors in the restoration of dance? God told David to "prepare a place for the ark." How does this parallel the importance of our "preparation" in dance ministry before we attempt to carry the presence of God in the dance? David finally concluded that, "None ought to carry the ark of God but the Levites." Can this speak of the principle that none ought to attempt to carry the presence of God through dance unless they are called of God and properly prepared? Have we, like David, taken too lightly the seriousness of following God's due order?

Final Thoughts

Every congregation has its own gestation period in the restoration of dance. It must not be foolishly rushed into and forced any more than it should be critically judged and denied. Due to a great lack of knowledge, the Church has suffered in either rejecting the dance or overzealously proceeding without knowledge or reverence. Balanced biblical understanding is necessary for the entire Church, whether you are called to a ministry in dance or not. There is a vast difference between being called to a ministry in dance and being a congregational worship dancer, yet dance (on many levels) is for anyone of any age who is willing to more freely express their worship to God. If what we truly seek is the pleasure, purpose, and presence of God in our worship, then we must be willing to follow God's blueprints concerning how these treasures are encountered. When our passion for God outweighs the comforts of man-made traditions, the true restoration process takes place. May the dance be built on a strong foundation, with an unshakeable knowledge of truth, that it may take its rightful place in worship, accomplishing God's original intent and purpose for His glory, honor, and power!

Dr. Ann Stevenson

For additional information about Dr. Ann Stevenson's ministry, "Restored to Glory Dance Ministry, School of Worship" including videos of her Dance Company, audio teachings, dance garments, and props, or to arrange for speaking/teaching engagements, contact:

Restored to Glory Dance Ministry
PO Box 1444
Bay City, MI 48706

Phone: 989-686-7937
Fax: 989-686-7937

WEBSITE :
www.danceministry.com

E-MAIL:
RTGDance@aol.com